God Speaks Science

Forget the Critics

by Gary Sutliff

God on Science

First Edition: December 2006
Second Edition: October 2009

Printed in the United States of America

Outline

God on Science

Preface:

I had some free time in the Summer of 2006 that God had graciously provided to me so I used it to gather notes on a subject near to my heart, real science, Bible science; the kind of science that is mesmerizing, fascinating and inspiring. I am grateful to my family who allowed me to pursue this endeavor and although I didn't finish until Christmas of 2006, it has truly been a fun endeavor. I have learned much, and praised God much as He would allow me to grow in understanding. I am deeply grateful to Dr. Chuck Missler who, in my opinion has been used by God to re-gain the scientific high ground within scripture more than anyone else in the past 100 years.

We serve an awesome God.

Gary Sutliff
Bond Servant of the Lord Jesus Christ

God on Science

Introduction 1.0

Listen – God is Speaking

Luke 24:31
"Heaven and earth will pass away, but My words will never pass away"
(NAS)

If the Word of God will never pass away, even though the universe as we know it will pass away, then we do know that the word contains eternal, perfect truth and is without errors. Otherwise, revisions would be in order as knowledge increased.

Psalm 111:2,10
"Great are the works of the Lord; they are studied by all who delight in them....the fear of the Lord is the beginning of wisdom."

A lot of good books about science and the bible have been written although I have yet to find one that isn't apologetic in nature. Apologetic works speak to seekers or critics of the Holy Scriptures attempting to validate scriptures via science. In this work, I have ignored the critics completely; I am not concerned with the ramblings of fools (God's term for those who don't believe in the existence of Him [Psalm 14:1]). Instead, I have taken the approach that God knows infinitely more than we have yet to discover, therefore, when He speaks, we should listen very seriously. And if we do, perhaps we might learn something beyond our current understanding. It is a shocking revelation to realize that this volume, called the Bible, contains 66 books written by 40 different authors over a period of 1,500 years and is 2,000 to 3,500 years old and speaks on several different scientific subjects, yet is without scientific error. In fact, many have argued against scriptural truth on the basis of scientific weakness. However, in contrast, we find that scientific discoveries of the past 100 years have substantially confirmed and validated the sacred scriptures rather than the reverse. As an example, the book that is believed to be the oldest of the recorded scriptures is Job contains marvelous scientific insights. In the last 3 chapters of Job, at least 15 shocking scientific revelations are made some of which have only been confirmed in the past 30 years.[1]

---

[1] See: "The Remarkable Record of Job", Henry M. Morris, Master Books, copyright 1988 and 2000, page 35

Are you a Christian? I mean a real I am going to heaven when I die Christian. Do you believe the God wrote the scriptures? Don't answer too fast. Most everyone who says that they are a Christian will say that God wrote the bible. That is not what I am asking. Do you believe that the scriptures are the actual words of God? For a searching skeptic, I have some really good news. God not only created this universe as we know it, but He has the ability to get a message to us. And, very importantly, so it can be discriminated from other false messages of would be gods and religions, the true God validated His message so we would know assuredly that it was from Him. By placing extensive prophetic information in the scriptures (The bible is 27% prophecy containing over 1,800 individual prophecies) [2] all of which has come to pass as timing has indicated (over ½ are still future) God has uniquely validated the Bible over all other religious writing of the world. This includes; the Book of Mormon, the Koran, the Vedas and all other pretenders for sacred scriptures. Back on point; now Christian, do you believe that the scriptures are the breath of God, as if directly spoken by Him? Think so?

> "He who can swim may bring up pearls from the depth of the sea, he who is unable to swim will be drowned, therefore only such persons as have had proper instruction should expose themselves to the risk." [3]

Very few Christians will take the stand that I have here. However, I don't stand alone but it is a small select group. Long ago, taking the position that scripture is the very breath of the Holy Spirit, and He is our teacher, I began to read the bible without caution and with a careless abandon began to look at the words of scripture. Fully accepting that the God of the universe is actually speaking these words to me, I began to look deep into pool of communication, with lingering thoughts of: "What is God saying?" "Why did He tell us that?" "What does this mean?" When the God who created all, speaks with even a casual reference to things of science, we can be confident that it is absolutely 100% scientifically accurate. In contrast to this approach, there are many good Christians today who will take the approach that the scriptures are valid only for spiritual understanding and not scientifically or historically correct. They say the bible is for saving of the soul, and what does saving of the soul have to

---

[2] "Encyclopedia of Biblical Prophecy"; J. Barton Payne; Baker Books; copyright 1973 – reprint 1980, 4th printing May 1997; page 674
[3] Maimonides – a Hebrew sage of the 12th century; "Guide of the Perplexed Part I – Maimonides" ; Translated by M. Friedlander; Hebrew Publishing Co. New York; first Published 1901; page 118

do with science and cosmology?" Well, I do agree that science is not the main point of the scriptures. After all it is true that if we were to gain mastery of the whole world but lose our eternal soul, we will have a net sum loss. However, I believe that God is so big, so smart, so knowledgeable, so consistent, so true and so righteous that when He speaks, it is not like a man. When God utters anything, it is

> **Everything Means Something**

absolutely true and without any deceit. So, I listen very carefully to what God says. I take what God says very seriously. Knowing that even in the subtleties of language, volumes are communicated. Not one dot of an "i", not one cross of a "t" is without meaning (Matt 5:18). Everything is said for a purpose and communicates a message to those who, by the Spirit of God, search diligently for understanding. As Chuck Missler has noted: "The rabbis have an expression that when the Messiah comes, He will not only interpret the passages and the words, but He will also interpret the letters, and not only the letters, but the spaces between the letters." I have found that this is not the ramblings of eccentric zealots, it is shockingly true.

So join me as we deep dive into the pool of scientific and engineering thoughts and phrases that God has spoken to us. The fools (those who chose to deny God's existence), Christian skeptics and those that just don't get it won't be there with us. But for those of you who take the time to make this journey, I guarantee that God will speak to you. Your eyes will become a little more open, and God.....and God.... will become bigger and bigger in your eyes. You will find praise flowing from your lips, and worship from your heart, and you will grow to know Him better and love Him more. Courage and faith will become more and more defining characteristics of you life.

Real Bible Science

Chapter 2.1

Formed in the Womb

Psalm1139:13-14 [other references: Jer 1:4-5; Isa 49:1-5]
*"For You formed my inward parts; **You wove me in my mother's womb**. I will give thanks to You, for I am fearfully and wonderfully made; Wonderful are Your works, and my soul knows it very well."* (NAS)

God orchestrates the forming of each one of us!

Formed (Hebrew - *qanah*); definition – to get, aquire ;Strong's #7069
Wove (Hebrew – *sakak*); definition – to weave together; Strong's #5526b

As the seed of the man (sperm) fertilizes the egg of the woman, life begins as a single cell. Approximately 24 hours later, this single cell divides into two identical cells referred to as Blastomeres in a division process called Mitosis.
Hours later, each of these two cells has divided into two more identical cells. Now there are 4 identical cells. The process is repeated a total of 4 times over a period of about 3 – 4 days until there are 16 identical cells. Each cell is exactly like its neighbor, 16 identical cells. Why aren't 16 babies developed from these 16 cells? Who tells each cell what to continue to develop until a heart forms, until an arm forms, until a leg forms? How does one cell know what the other cells are doing? How is this orchestrated? Who is making the decisions? An analogy is an orchestra. If we got 50 people together, each who could play a number of instruments, we

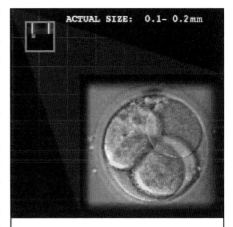

Human cells in initial stage of life development (Blastomeres)

still have no music. Who assigns the people to their station? Even if the people were somehow assigned, who leads them to function together? How do they interact?

In engineering, this problem is referred to as "Conflict Resolution" and is encountered in all computer and some mechanical systems. Another example:

what if 9 people join together to play a game of softball. Who decides who plays where? What about the batting order, who will work that out? All systems require a person in charge making the decisions, orchestrating the process to some eventual end.

In a shocking revelation, God informs us that He is actively involved in the individual and personal development of each one of our lives. He is the orchestra leader, the one calling the shots. This is eye opening at two levels at least. (1) Biological: Development of an infant baby requires input from outside the mother. This addresses the question of why 16 identical cells don't turn into 16 babies and how the 1,000's of other decisions that are required leading the process of forming a child can be made. Input from the outside is required and God provides it. (2) Development of an infant is not a random process! God is actively involved in the process of "weaving" us together. He is the one who "forms" us in the womb of our mothers. The implication is that God's involvement in our personal life is active, detailed, persistent, and critical. We are made exactly the way God chose us to be. We are not the result of some random chance development. It is not simply a mater of dominate and weaker genes. We are the result of God's deliberate actions.

As we ponder this truth, its implications become staggering. The same thoughts are also echoed in Jeremiah 1:4-5 *"Now the word of the Lord came to me saying, 'Before I formed you in the womb I knew you, and before you were born I consecrated you; I have appointed you a prophet to the nations."* See also Isaiah 49:1-5

Chapter 2.2

Miracle of DNA

Ps 139:13-16

*"For Thou didst form my inward parts; Thou didst weave me in my mother's womb. I will give thanks to Thee, for I am fearfully and wonderfully made; Wonderful are Thy works, and my soul knows it very well. My frame was not hidden from Thee, when I was made in secret, and skillfully wrought in the depths of the earth. **Thine eyes have seen my unformed substance**; and in Thy book they were all written, the days that were ordained for me when as yet there was not one of them...."* (NAS)

DNA in the Bible?

Unformed Substance (Hebrew *golem*); definition ; *"something rolled together*; hence *rude* and *unformed matter*, not yet wrought, the parts of which are not yet unfolded and developed, thus and embryo." [4]   Strong's #1564

This verse is fabulously provocative giving us a shocking insight to God's level of involvement in our personal lives by highlighting His oversight of us even at initial cell formation. God's is actively involved in our physical formation and scripture uses a word that seems to indicate or at least anticipate DNA.   DNA is that fascinating substance that is the "blueprint" in essence that uniquely defines exactly who each one of us is. The entire biological and scientific community was shocked by the

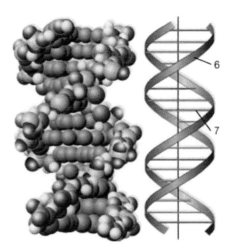

discovery in the 1950's by Francis Crick, James Watson and Maurice Wilkins of this little micro mechanism that is used to carry our very unique genetic makeup from our initial first cell to all the subsequent cells that will

---

[4] http://www.blueletterbible.org/tmp_dir/words/1/1158857960-3467.html

grow to make up our bodies. Recent CSI television shows have brought to the forefront how important and individualistic each persons DNA really is. An analogy is often used to help understand the complexity of DNA. If someone was to take 125 miles of mono-filament fishing line and squeeze it into a basketball it would represent a scaled version of the actual DNA structure. DNA is actually packed in every cell in something the size of the head of a pin and when unspooled and stretched out, it measures over 6 feet. Absolutely amazing, and oh by the way, every time the cell divides, this long strand of DNA is duplicated in a most intricate way. It starts in effect by doubling its width, unrolls or spools out and then zippers itself apart forming two strands of the double helix DNA and then spooling back in. Our very first cell, which is the product of fertilization, defines our entire genetic make-up and is a combination of the DNA from our mother's embryo and our father's sperm. It would appear from Psalm 139:16 that God is already involved at this point.

**At the moment of conception,
a fertilized human egg is about the size of a pinhead.
Yet it contains information equivalent to about six billion "chemical letters."
This is enough information to fill 1000 books,
500 pages thick with print so small you would need a microscope to read it!**

Verse 16 uses Hebrew word *golem* which is translated into "substance" (KJV) or "unformed substance" (NIV & NAS). *Golem* has been difficult to translate and is only use one time in the entire bible which is here. Many suggest embryo is the intended meaning of the word but Strong's points out that *golem* is derived from the root word *galam* which means; "to wrap up, fold, or fold together" [5] or "rolled together" [6] which is tantalizing familiar in sounding to the process of DNA being duplicated in the spooling out, zippering and spooling back up.

---

[5] "Zondervan NASB Exhaustive Concordance"; Zondervan; copyright 1981 & 2000; page 1378
[6] See Blue Letter Bible:
http://www.blueletterbible.org/tmp_dir/words/1/1158857960-3467.html

Genetic Confirmation of Biblical Accounts: *Did Adam know Eve?*

A mind-blowing revelation from the field of Genetic Anthropology (which is the study of man's ancestry through genetic DNA) came as two elements of DNA are studied using: the Y-chromosome for male line history and mitochondrial DNA for female line history. It turns out that there is a surprising insight as mankind's DNA is traced back to its origin. What was discovered

is that the first man (or better stated the male point of common origin) was many generations **after** the first woman (female point of common origin). This discovery in the 1980's gave rise to the occasion in the scientific community to proclaim that "Adam" never knew "Eve". Apparently, Eve significantly preceded Adam. Specifically speaking, the DNA record shows that all men of the earth have a single common male ancestor and all women have a single common female ancestor but the common female was many generations before the common male. This remains a significant mystery to the scientific community even today as they claim that Adam never knew Eve.[7] As deep a mystery that this is to the scientific community, even grade school students of the Bible can solve this dilemma. Genesis tells us of the real Adam and Eve who were the source or parents of all the living (Genesis 3:20; *"Eve...the mother of all the living"*). However, we also learn from Genesis 7-9 that only eight people survived the flood of Noah. Specifically Noah, his wife, his three sons and their respective three wives. [By the way, most people have trouble identifying Noah's wife. I can clear up this mystery, it is Joan! Surely you have heard of "Joan of Ark". Anyway] Noah was the father of his three sons and all mankind descended from him as the common male ancestor. Noah's wife however, was not the mother of all; there were three other women present on the ark who were not Noah's descendents (the son's wives). Therefore, to find a common mother, genetic history can be traced all the way back to Eve, who, and no one can say it

---

[7] This can be seen an article in "News in Science" relays the thought of Eve preceding Adam.
http://www.abc.net.au/science/news/stories/s206915.htm

better that Jesus, was the mother of all living. So, we find that Genetic Anthropology through DNA has given an external verification of both Adam, Eve and the chronicle of Noah's flood. Astounding!

Discovery Channel aired a program several years back based on this information. Genetic anthropologists concluded from this and other data that the ancient world which had grown to a very large population had at that time experienced a dramatic reduction of life to something approximating 28 people. Secular scientists speculated on the nature of the catastrophe including everything from asteroid strikes, ice age, and comet strikes; everything but the real answer. Once again, a mystery to modern scientists can be easily solved by our grade school Sunday School student. Noah's flood easily accounts for and anticipates this dilemma, although it was only 8 people who survived. Some Christian scientists have suggested pre-flood populations ranging from several hundred million to several billion.

The Days of Your Life are Fixed!

Psalm 139:16 "Your eyes saw my unformed body. *__All the days ordained for me were written in your book before one of them came to be__*." (NIV)

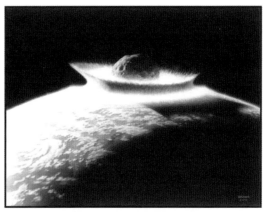

In spite of efforts by some to change it, the death rate remains at 100%. Physical death will come upon us all and it is surprising to learn that indeed, "our days are numbered." Verse 16 indicates that our very days are ordained for us and DNA research has revealed the mechanism by which this occurs and thereby have confirmed that the length of our very life is pre-programmed and therefore, pre-ordained. "Apparently, this is caused by a mechanism in the DNA involving a repetitive DNA sequence which is at the end of each chromosome called a telomere. Part of the telomere is shaved off with every cell division; its complete removal initiates cell suicide thereby limiting the number of cell divisions possible. Now this doesn't address the bullfighter that doesn't make it to the end of the event but it is provocative in that our physical lives are individually limited.

Jewish Applications in DNA Research:

Also of interest is the identification of a DNA marker referred to as the Cohen Modal Haplotype (CMH), which is distinct among Jewish men who claim to be descendants of Aaron the High Priest. Genetic analysis places the original possessor of the CHM to a time frame around 3,300 years ago, which corresponds very closely to the biblical dating of Aaron. Another fascinating development is a gathering that is being billed as "The Biggest Family Reunion of All Time, 3,000 Years in the Making." Organizers intend to gather all the males who claim to be descendants of King David's line and activities will include mass DNA testing. Could this possibly provide someone justification to claim to be the Messiah? [8]

"At that moment, when the DNA/RNA system became understood, the debate between Evolutionists and Creationists should have come to a screeching halt".......
I.L. Cohen, Researcher and Mathematician; Member NY Academy of Sciences; Officer of the Archaeological Inst. of America

---

[9]

Stringing Together the Big Picture:

We are chosen before the foundation of the world.

Eph 1:3-4 *"Blessed be the God and Father of our Lord Jesus Christ, who has blessed us with every spiritual blessing in the heavenly places in Christ, just as* ***He chose us in Him before the foundation of the world***, *that we should be holy and blameless before Him. In love"* (NAS)

Works are prepared for us in advance to do
Eph 2:10 *"For we are His workmanship, created in Christ Jesus for good works, which* ***God prepared beforehand***, *that we should walk in them."* (NAS)

God oversees our development from even at the embroy level.
Ps 139:16 *"Thine eyes have* ***seen my unformed substance***; *and in Thy book they were all written, the days that were ordained for me when as yet there was not one of them."* (NAS)

---

[8] Data comes from an excellent and fascinating article by Wendy Wipple published by Konoinia House: "Written for a Generation to Come."
[9] As quoted by ChristianAnswers.net, http://www.christiananswers.net/q-eden/origin-of-life.html

The purpose or the meaning of life is to be with God in heaven.

2 Cor 5:2-8 *"For indeed in this house we groan, longing to be clothed with our dwelling from heaven; inasmuch as we, having put it on, shall not be found naked. For indeed while we are in this tent, we groan, being burdened, because we do not want to be unclothed, but to be clothed, in order that what is mortal may be swallowed up by life. Now **He who prepared us for this very purpose is God**, who gave to us the Spirit as a pledge. Therefore, being always of good courage, and knowing **that while we are at home in the body we are absent from the Lord**-- for we walk by faith, not by sight-- we are of good courage, I say, and prefer rather to be absent from the body and to be at home with the Lord."* (NAS)

Big Picture: Before God made the heavens and earth, He conceived us and chose us. He brought His selected DNA from our father and combined it with that of our mother and oversaw and directed every aspect of our development in the womb so that we are completely and uniquely the way God intended us to be. He lovingly created a path for us to walk in this life. One that brings us joy and fulfillment as we do the good works prepared in advance for us. And one day, when the days that God has ordained for us on this earth are complete, we will join God in the heavens. It is for this purpose we were created. It is for this reason that God made us. To live in loving relationship with Him, of our own free choice, which is only the way true love is available. This life is full of trials, ordained by God for our benefit, but one day, when we have completed our course, we will live with God and the cares and worries of this life will be over. There will be no more death, no more crying, nor more pain, no more tears and no more sorrow. We will drink deeply from the spring of the water of life, without cost (Rev 21:4-6).

Chapter 2.3

Medicine and Hygiene

Exodus 15:26
"If you will give earnest heed to the voice of the LORD your God, and do what is right in His sight, and give ear to His commandments, and keep all His statutes, **_I will put none of the diseases on you which I have put on the Egyptians; for I the LORD, am your healer_**." (NAS)

God is interested in your health
213 out of 613 biblical commandments found in the Torah (first 5 books of the Bible) are detailed medical regulations that insured the good health of the children of Israel if they would obediently follow the laws of God.

Egyptian Papyrus
S.E. Massengill translated the Papyrus Ebers (estimated to be dated at 1552 B.C.) which contained pharmaceutical descriptions that were in common use in Egypt at the time Moses scribed the first five books of the Old Testament (the Exodus was about 1445 BC [10]). Egypt's medicines contained the following as main ingredients; Lizards blood, swine's teeth, putrid meat, stinking fat, moisture from pigs ears, milk, goose grease, asses' hoofs, animal fats from various sources, excreta from animals including human beings, donkeys, antelopes, dogs, cats and even flies. [11]

An example of Egyptian medical ignorance and primitive state of their knowledge is the doctor's suggestion for healing an infected splinter wound. The prescription involves the application of an ointment mixture composed of the blood of worms mixed with the dung of a donkey.

Hygienic guidance of the scriptures stands in stark contrast to the Egyptian "wisdom of the world."

---

[10] "The Bible Exposition Commentary – OT – Gen-Deut"; Warren Wiersbe; Victor – Cook Communication; copyright 2001; Page 185
[11] Much of this information is contained in "None of These Diseases"; S. I .McMillen, M.D.; Spire Books – Revell; copyright 1963, 13th printing Sept 1972

Egyptian writing on papyrus
(above)
Papyrus plant (below)

Papyrus Fragments

Black Plague

The "Dark Ages" became especially black during the 14th Century when the Black Death reigned. In that century alone, it is estimated that one out of every three people lost their lives generating a death count of over 60 million. It was one of the greatest disasters ever recorded in human history. "Sweeping everything before it, this plague brought panic and confusion in its train...The dead were hurled pell-mell into huge pits, hastily dug for the purpose, and putrefying bodies lay about everywhere in the houses and streets." [12] As doctors tried to stem the rising tide of death, they offered the ridiculous advice like "Stop eating pepper or garlic".

"He shall remain unclean all the days during which he has the infection; he is unclean. ***He shall live alone****; his dwelling shall be* ***outside the camp****."* Lev 13:46

---

[12] From "History of Medicine"; Fielding Garrison; Saunders; 1929; page 63-65; as quoted in "None of these Diseases"; page 11

In Vienna a statue stands in the middle of the city dedicated to the Black Death's victims and the actions of the church fathers who were credited with bringing the plague to an end.[13] Wise church leaders eventually turned to God for help and found that Leviticus 13:46 contained detailed information of plague victims, which included washing and quarantining (not a common practice in any previous society). The people of Europe adopted the laws given to Moses in the ancient past and God answered their prayers and brought an end to the scourge of the Black Death.

---

[13] "The Signature of God", Grant R. Jeffrey, Frontier Research Pub., copyright 1996, Page 149

Doctors Washing their Hands?

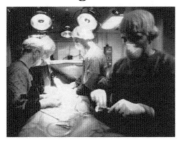 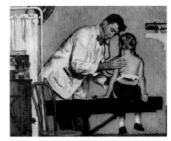

A brilliant Hungarian doctor , Dr. Ignaz Semmelweis, in 1847 discovered that washing the hands of doctors between patient examinations significantly reduced that transmission of diseases from patients in hospitals.   At Allegemeine Krakenhause, Vienna's premiere teaching hospital, it was the practice of the doctors and their students in the maternity ward of the sick to begin their day by examining the patients who had died the previous night and then, without washing their hands, to conduct pelvic exams of the sick pregnant women. They went from patient to patient without ever washing their hands our using rubber gloves. Their mortality rate was 1 out of every 6 women died before leaving the hospital. Germs were not to be identified until many years later, but by observation, Dr. Semmelweis noted the connection between the exams and patients deaths. He instituted a mandate requiring that all doctors wash their hands between patient exams.   This resulted in the mortality rate dropping in the first month to 1 in 42 (from previously 1 in 6) and within a few months, it had drooped to 1 in 84. [14]

The statistics of improvement don't shock us today but another facet to the story that is of interest is the reaction of the Medical Community to this practice. Not wanting to be bothered by the inconvenience of washing hands, Semmelweis was constantly ridiculed and eventually fired from the hospital because no one could believe that something was passed from one patient to the other that couldn't be seen.

In 1958 a Staphylococcus infection spread rapidly through a hospital that was caused by improperly washed hands. Various antibiotics of the time were of little help, and before the infection was brought under control it snuffed out the lives of 86 men, women and children. The New Your State Department of Health became so alarmed at the speed of the spread of the infection that in

---

[14] "None of these Diseases"; page 14

1960 they issued a book describing a method of washing the hands. "…and the procedures closely approximate the Scriptural method given in Numbers 19. At long last, in the year 1960, man finally muddled through. He learned, after centuries and at a frightful cost, what God gave to Moses by inspiration."[15]

Numbers 19:11-22 (partial)
"The one who touches the corpse of any person shall be unclean for seven days. That one shall purify himself from uncleanness with the water on the third and seventh day, and then he shall be clean....anyone who in the open field touches on who has been slain with a sword or who has died naturally, or a human bone or a grave, shall be unclean for seven days....Furthermore, ___anything that the unclean person touches shall be unclean; and the person who touches it shall be unclean___ *until evening."*

Most germs deposited by a touch, cough or sneeze will die on the surface they come in contract with usually within 2-6 hours depending on temperature and humidity.

Circumcision:
25% of all cancer in women is of the cervix. In 1954 a study of over 86,000 women in Boston revealed that cervical cancer in non-Jewish women was 8 ½ times greater than in Jewish women. "Medical researchers agree that this spectacular freedom results from the practice of circumcision in Jewish men – which God ordered Abraham to institute four thousand years ago." [16]

Photo of circumcision not shown for multiple reasons.

Genesis 17:11-12
"And ___you shall be circumcised___ *in the flesh of your foreskin, and it shall be the sign for the covenant between Me and you. And every male among you who is eight days old shall be circumcised throughout you generations."*

---

[15] "None of these Diseases"; page 16
[16] "None of these Diseases"; page 18

Cost of Free Sex:

1 Corinthians 10:8, 11

*"We should not **commit sexual immorality, as some of them did, and in one day twenty-three thousand of them died**....These things happened to them as examples and were written down as warnings for us, on whom te fulfillment of the ages has come."*

- **25 million people have died of AIDS since 1981**
- **It is the most destructive epidemic in history**
- **3.1 million died in 2005 alone**
- **8,500 deaths per year currently**
- **Estimated 40.3 million people living with AIDS today**

The cost of AIDS, syphilis, herpes, gonorrhea and other sexually transmitted diseases (STD's) on our society and planet is so great it can not be measured. It all could all come to an end, be completely wiped out in one generation, if we only could learn from the example of those who have gone before us.

"If history has taught us anything, it is that man learns nothing from history."

Peace in the Human Body:

Philippians 4:6

*"**Be anxious for nothing**, but in everything by prayer an supplication, with thanksgiving let you requests be made known to God. And the peace of God, which surpasses all comprehension, shall guard you hearts and your minds in Christ Jesus"*

Dr. S.I. McMillen; "No one can appreciate so fully as a doctor the amazingly large percentage of human disease and suffering which is directly traceable to worry, fear, conflict, immorality, dissipation, and ignorance – to unwholesome thinking and unclean living. The sincere acceptance of the principles and teachings of Christ with respect to the life of mental peace and joy, the life of unselfish thought and clean

> **Worry is an expression of a lack of faith, and, it takes a toll on health. Trusting in God results in a peace which is beyond our comprehension.**

living, would at once wipe out more than half the difficulties, diseases, and sorrows of the human race. In other words, more than one half of the present affliction of mankind could be prevented by the tremendous prophylactic power of actually living up to the personal and practical spirit of the real teachings of Christ.

The teaching of Jesus applied to our modern civilization – understandingly applied, not merely nominally accepted – would so purify, uplift, and vitalize us that the race would immediately stand out as a new order of beings, possessing superior mental power and increased moral force. Irrespective of the future rewards of living, laying aside all discussion of future life, it would pay any man or woman to live the Christ-life just for the mental and moral rewards it affords here in this present world." [17]

---

[17] "None of these Diseases"; page 64-65

2 – Medical and Personal

Chapter 2.4

Human Chemical Makeup

Genesis 2:7
"*Then the LORD God **formed man of dust from the ground**, and breathed into his nostrils the breath of life; and man became a living being.*" (NAS)

Genesis 3:19
"*By the sweat of your face, you will eat bread, **till you return to the ground, because from it you were taken; for you are dust, and to dust you shall return**.*"

Formed: (Hebrew: *yatsar*) definition: to form, fashion, frame – Strong's #3335
Dust: (Hebrew: `*aphar*) definition: dry earth, dust, powder, ashes, earth, ground, mortar, rubbish – Strong's #6083

Lump of Clay:

A 1982 *Reader's Digest* article (Nov 1982) described a fascinating discovery by the researchers at NASA's Ames Research Center which stated that clay and earth contain every single element found in the human body. Specifically, we are composed of the following elements, all found in the ground:

Organic Building Blocks		Salts		Trace Elements	
Total	96.2%	Total	3.9%	Total	< 0.5%
Oxygen	65.0%	Calcium	1.5%	Chromium	Trace
Carbon	18.5%	Phosphorus	1.0%	Cobalt	Trace
Hydrogen	9.5%	Potassium	0.4%	Copper	Trace
Nitrogen	3.2%	Sulfur	0.3%	Fluorine	Trace
		Sodium	0.2%	Manganese	Trace
		Chlorine	0.2%	Molybdenum	Trace
		Magnesium	0.1%	Selenium	Trace
		Iodine	0.1%	Tin	Trace
		Iron	0.1%	Vanadium	Trace
				Zinc	Trace

Isaiah 45:9 *"Woe to the one who quarrels with his Maker-- An earthenware vessel among the vessels of earth! Will the clay say to the potter, 'What are you doing?' Or the thing you are making say, 'He has no hands'?"*

Twila Paris has a song with a phrase that captures the thought:

> **What am I, but a piece of earth;**
> **Breathing holy breath;**
> **What am I without You?**

Chapter 2.5

Evolution vs Creation

Genesis 2:7
"Then the LORD God formed man of dust from the ground, and breathed into his nostrils the breath of life, and man became a living being." (NAS)

Romans 1: 22, 25
"Professing to be wise, they became fools...exchanging the truth of God for a lie, and worshipped and served the creature rather than the Creator who is blessed forever."
[18]

"If a small glass ball (marble) is found in the woods needs a cause, then making the ball bigger does not eliminate the need for a cause"

Ramblings of Fools

Stephen Jay Gold:
Quoted Psalm 8 then stated; "Darwin removed this keystone of false comfort more than a century ago, but many people still believe that they cannot navigate this vale of tears without such a crutch." [19]

Christians, we are not in a debate, we are in a war and the high ground is the validity of the Holy Scriptures.

Creation
vs
Evolution

---

[18] Richard Taylor; as quoted in "Systematic Theology – Vol 1"; Norman Giesler; page 177
[19] Science Magazine – Editorial; June 25, 1999

Fossils

It was stated by evolutionists early on in the development of the theory (late 1800's) that as more and more fossils were discovered, intermediary species would be found. Intermediary species are the animals that are the transition animals from on species to another, more advanced species, as viewed by the evolutionists. In Charles Darwin's time, there were very few fossils and it generally thought that when more were discovered, and abundance of intermediary species would be found.

The British Museum of Natural History houses the world's largest fossil collection, containing over 60 million specimens. Colin Patterson, a senior paleontologist at the museum stated; "If I knew of any [evolutionary transitions], fossil or living, I would certainly have included them [in my book *Evolution*]."[20] David Raup is the curator of the Field Museum of Natural History in Chicago. He stated; "We are now about 120 years after Darwin and the knowledge of the fossil record has been greatly expanded. We now have a quarter of a million fossil species, but the situation hasn't changed much...**We have even fewer**

examples of evolutionary transition than we had in Darwin's time." [21] Newsweek, in an article summarizing the sentiments of leading evolutionists at a conference in Chicago stated; "Evidence from fossils now points overwhelmingly away from the classical Darwinism which most Americans learned in high school." [22] David Raup; "...During the past few years...you have experienced a shift from evolution as knowledge to evolution as faith...Evolution not only conveys no knowledge, but seems somehow to convey anti-

---

[20] "Those Fossils are a Problem", Answers in Genesis, http://www.answersingenesis.org/creation/v14/i4/fossils.asp (September 1992)
[21] "Invertebrates: animals without backbones", Dr. Gary Parker, Answers In Genesis, http://www.answersingenesis.org/home/area/cfol/ch3-invertebrates.asp
[22] As quoted in "Sensible Science", Dr. Bert Thompson and Dr. Brad Harrub, http://www.apologeticspress.org/articles/2088

knowledge." [23]

Some examples of known species with no supporting intermediary species include the dolphin and sea horse. The dolphin finds food by sonar and the sea horse is a marsupial but the father carries the young. A very significant problem for evolutionists is the path from lizard to bird. A mythical bird Archaeopteryx has been proposed but no evidence in the fossil record has provided any real supporting evidence although claims are made to the contrary. In fact, several intentional frauds have been perpetrated upon the scientific community in this area.

Because of the difficulty with classical evolutionary theory, newer theories have emerged to help solve the problem. One is **Punctuated Equilibrium**, which believes that new species evolved in large, quick jumps. Another theory is **Intelligent Design**, supported by some biological scientists that believe an "intelligent agency" must have been involved in some stage of life's origin and dispersal.

Ape Men

Although many scientists are moral reasonable folks, in the field of anthropology, the search of the "missing link" is so littered with the trash and debris of conscious, perpetrated frauds it has given science a major black eye. Of importance is that these frauds have not been secondary findings but have served as key evolutionary validating evidences and even after the deception has been exposed, they continue to be use as

---

[23] "Evolution is a Religion", Creation Worldview Ministries,
http://www.creationworldview.org/articles_view.asp?id=89

validating examples. For your review:[24]

⇨ **Java Man** – Homo erectus
  ▪ A skullcap and three teeth were found on Java in 1891 by Eugene Dubois
  ▪ The femur was found fifty feet from the skullcap a full year later
  ▪ For 30 years he downplayed the fact that he also found two human skulls in close proximity
  ▪ An extensive fact finding expedition (Selenka Expedition) was conducted on Java man by 19th century evolutionists for the purpose of validating the claims
  ▪ However the 342 page scientific report from the expedition demonstrates beyond a doubt that Java man played no part in human evolution
  ▪ Incredibly, Time magazines article "How Man Began" (14 Mar 1994) treated Java Man as a true ancestor and some advocate that it be included as one of the five "truths of evolution"
  ▪ It is however complete fiction

⇨ **Piltdown Man**

  ▪ A skull and a jaw bone were found by Lawyer - Charles Dawson in 1912
  ▪ Piltdown man was declared the common ancestor of Neanderthal and modern man
  ▪ In 1953 Piltdown Man was discovered to be and was subsequently declared a fraud
  ▪ It is a human skull with an ape jawbone that was stained and filed to match
  ▪ Notorious scientific fraud

⇨ **Peking Man**

  ▪ A tooth was discovered by Davidson Black who was about to run out of exploration funds in 1927 and Peking Man was born
  ▪ Within 10 years 14 skulls (no skeletons) had been found (all bashed at the base)
  ▪ Subsequently they have been identified as monkey skulls, yet, Peking man still lives
  ▪ Skulls eventually "disappeared"
  ▪ Fantasy

Peking Man – Plaster Cast reconstruction

---

[24] For background see: "The Face That Demonstrates the Farce of Evolution", Hank Hanegraaff, Word Publishing, copyright 1998, Pages 49-60

⇨ **Bomb Shell**
  - Dr. Richard Leaky Jr. discovered a skull in 1972
  - The modern looking skull was dated at two different locations and determined to be 1.5 and 2.5 million years old
  - Richard Leakey stated himself: "What we have discovered simply wipes out everything we have ever been taught on evolution and I have nothing to offer in its place."

The Missing Link is still missing and the available information is clearly tainted.

Chance of Spontaneous Life

There is a concept referred to as "Irreducible Complexity" which states that an entire mechanism must be formed together in order for the item to work. An example is a simple mouse trap. It has only five basic parts: spring, platform, hammer, catch and latch however, even though each part is simple by itself, the device cannot function without all the five parts being in place.

"Simple" – One Cell Organisms

2 – Medical and Personal

- Tiny bacterial cells consist of 100 Billion atoms
- More complex than any machine built by man
- It posses the capacity of information storage, control systems, manufacturing systems, metabolic systems, error correction and several other things
- Flagellum are the little hair like strands that extend from the organism. This little one cell organism rotates each flagellum in order to propel itself forward.
- Not surprising, the Flagellum require 40 different parts just in themselves to function

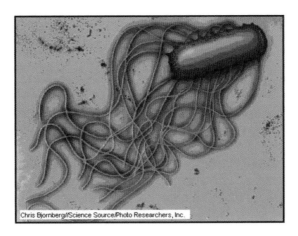

Chris Bjornberg//Science Source/Photo Researchers, Inc.

Molecular biologist Michael Denton states: "Although the tiniest bacterial cells are incredibly small,…each is in effect a veritable micro-miniaturized factory containing thousands of exquisitely designed pieces of intricate molecular machinery….far more complicated than any machine built by man and is absolutely without parallel in the non-living world" [25]

Even though many make a great deal about the 1953 Stanley Miller graduate student experiments who formed a simple amino acid in a test setup, most objective scientists see little value in the experiment. Evolutionists Robert Shapiro comments: "The very best …chemistry…doesn't not take us very far along the path to a living organism. The chemicals…no more resembles a bacterium than a small pile of real and nonsense words, that written on an individual scrap of paper resembles the complete works of Shakespeare"

---

[25] Evolution: A Theory in Crisis"; Michael Denton, summary at:
http://www.forananswer.org/Top_Ath/Michael%20Denton.pdf

Odds of Spontaneous Life:

- Harold Morowitz, Yale University physicist, estimated that the odds of a single bacterium re-assembling by chance is one in $10^{100,000,000,000}$.
- Applying this, we find that it is more likely that you and your entire family would win the state lottery every week for a million years than for a bacterium to form by chance!
- Scientists consider odds of 10^{50} absurd
- DNA
    - Probability of a single strand of DNA occurring on its own is 10^{130}
    - Assuming the earth is 15 billion years old, we have 10^{18} seconds
    - Scientists estimate the total number of atoms in the universe is 10^{70}
- Jar of Peanut Butter; Example
    - The food industry relies on the impossibility of new life by biogenesis. Over a billion experiments per year have been conducted for over a century!
    - Biogenesis is not unlikely, it is impossible!
- Chance
    - Nobel Laureate, George Wald (Harvard); "One has to only contemplate the magnitude of this task to concede that the spontaneous generation of a living organism is impossible. Yet we are here as a result, I believe, of spontaneous generation" 1954
    - Francis Crick, Nobel Prize in biology for DNA; "An honest man, armed with all the knowledge available to us now, could only state than in some sense, the origin of life appears at the moment to be almost a miracle" 1982

[26]

> **"..It is logically impossible to ascribe *any power* to chance whatsoever."**

---

[26] "Not a Chance"; R.C.Sproul; Baker Books; copyright 1994; 2nd printing March 2000; page xiv

Sutliff's Challenge

Rock brought back from Mars?!?!

I pose the following problem as an illustration that God must exist. Imagine that a future space probe was to return to Earth from a journey to Mars and it brought back with it the object shown above. I would venture to suggest that every person, including scientists, would make strong arguments that this would prove that there was once life on Mars. After all, someone or thing must have created the object we see before us. It is only logical to see something with order and conclude that there is a designer and maker behind the object. I propose that even this simple wedge with symbols on it would become the "evidence" that would be used to emphatically prove that there is or at least was, life on Mars. My guess is that even those who emphatically wish to deny the existence of God, will with this simplistic object, make a case for Martian life.

I assert that we ourselves are a greater creation than a wedge with symbols. To suggest that we are not the result of a creator is illogical.

Jesus on who God is:

Jesus was questioned by a group of people (Sadducees) who didn't believe in life after death. When asked about this issue Jesus responded, "*I am the God of Abraham, and the God of Isaac, and the God of Jacob'? He is **not the God of the dead but of the living**.*" Matt 22:32 (NAS)

Summary

Evolution: It is truly a "Theory in Crisis" [27] and those left who continue to support it are clearly converts to the religion of humanism. They have consciously ignored clear scientific facts and archeological evidence and they are substantially lacking in objective common sense. They have willfully turned away from God. As Romans 1 clearly states; "*Professing to be wise, they became fools...exchanging the truth of God for a lie, and worshipped and served the creature rather than the Creator.*" This should not come as a surprise to Christians because Peter (2 Pet 3:3-6) prophetically warns us that the rejection of a Creator God is a sign of the end times.

> **Darwinists have little to show for 140 years of research by thousands of scientists spending millions of dollars**

> **The emperor has no clothes and people are beginning to notice**

---

[27] See also: "*Darwin's Black Box*"; Michael Behe; "*Darwin on Trial*"; Phillip Johnson; "*Evolution: A theory In Crisis*"; Michael Denton

2 – Medical and Personal

Chapter 2.6

Bandwidth of God

Psalm 139:17-18

"How precious also are Your thoughts to me, O God! How vast is the sum of them! **_If I should count them, they would outnumber the sand_**. *When I awake, I am still with You."* (NAS)

Thought (Hebrew – *rea*) definition: purpose, aim, thought – Strong's #7454
Count (Hebrew – *caphar*) definition: count or enumerate – Strong's #5608
Outnumber (Hebrew – *rabah*) definition: become great, become numerous, become many or much – Strong's #7235
Sand (Hebrew – *chowl*) definition: sand – Strong's #2344

What is the Bandwidth of God?

It is absolutely staggering and shocking to realize the depth and extent of God's involvement and interest in our lives. I have heard many times people say, "well, I don't want to bother God with this" or "I don't think God has the time", or "I don't think God cares about this." Basically, this all boils down to God is not big enough or capable enough or interested enough for the small stuff. Yes, maybe if my life is in immediate danger God cares but He certainly isn't interested in the fact that someone just spoke harshly to me and my feelings are hurt and it bothers me. Well, Psalm 139:17-18 delivers a different message. On one hand, we could take God's words in Psalm 139 as a simple hyperbole. This would mean that God simply thinks of us a lot. However, if we look at God's words more seriously, we get further insight.

The number of thoughts, the rate at which God is thinking about us and is focused on us is alarming. I am probably a rather self focused, self centered person and I find myself thinking about myself rather often. In fact, I would say that on average, I think about myself once every 15 minutes or so. I probably think about myself 100 times a day. That's a lot, isn't it? Well, it may be a lot but not nearly as much as God is thinking about us. If God's thoughts of us are like the sand on the beach, His depth of knowledge and involvement in our lives is beyond comprehension. Consider the following: Size of a grain of sand: [28]

---

[28] http://ask.metafilter.com/mefi/42777

- 1.0 - 2.0mm - Very Coarse Sand
- 0.5 - 1.0mm - Coarse Sand
- 0.25 - 0.5mm - Medium Sand
- 0.125 - 0.25mm - Fine Sand
- 0.05 - 0.125mm - Very Fine Sand

0.25	Size of grain of sand (mm)
50	Width of Beach (m)
1	Depth of Sand (m)
1,500,000	Length of Coast line (km)
4.8E+21	Grains of Sand
72	Life span years
2.27E+09	Time in Sec
2.11E+12	**Thoughts/second**

Using an average of sand size of 0.25mm, with an average shore width of sand (50m) and an average depth of sand of 1m and knowing that there are about 1.5 million km (almost 1 million miles) we find that there are about 4.8 10^{21} total grains of sand on the earth. This is a huge number. This is also a rather conservative estimate recognizing that there is sand on the ocean floor, and sand in land areas (such as the desert). If you lived to an age of 72 years old, your life span would only be 2.27 10^{9} seconds. If we divide these two numbers together, we find that Gods thoughts of each one of us are 2.11 10^{12} times per second!! Did you get that? That is 2 trillion times per second!! That is intensive frequency and bandwidth. God is so into each one of us it is difficult to comprehend. God is thinking about us, about every aspect of our lives at a rate that vastly extends beyond what we think of ourselves.

> **God thinks of each of us over 2 trillion times every second of every hour of every day!**

Can you imagine the capability of God, if He is tracking each person on the planet, tracking perhaps 10^{21} angels, tracking all those who have gone before us at a level of 2 trillion times per second!! It is truly incomprehensible. Please don't ever say, God does not have the time or interest in what ever you are thinking about. He does and Psalm 139 indicates that He cares perhaps more than you do.

Hairs on Your Head?

If you are having difficulty with this concept, and don't believe that God is really into us at that level, I have some more bad news. Consider the following:

Jesus tells us in Matthew 10:29-31 (see also Luke 12:7 and Luke 21:18):

"Are not two sparrows sold for a cent? And yet not one of them will fall to the ground apart from your Father. ***But the very hairs of your head are all numbered****. So do not fear; you are more valuable than many sparrows."*

Jesus tells us that the very hairs on our head are numbered! Wow! This gives us the following insights:

> **Most people have about 90,000 to 140,000 hairs. We lose about 50 to 100 hairs per day. Many of mine are already gone.**

- In my whole life, I never thought it of any value to count the number of hairs on my head (even though I am now at 55 becoming rather bald) yet God tracks that level of detail in my life
- If God knows this level of detail in my life, He certainly must know everything that I can think of that would be important, or even trivial.
- The number of hairs on my head is changing constantly (losing somewhere between 50 and 100 per day [29]). God's interest in me is current, active, immediate and extremely detailed.

---

[29] See: http://kidshealth.org/kid/health_problems/skin/hair_loss.html

31

2 – Medical and Personal

Chapter 3.1

Beginning of Time

Genesis 1:1 – See also John 9:32
"In the beginning God created the heavens and the earth." (NAS)

Jude 25
*"...to the only God our Savior, through Jesus Christ our Lord, be glory, majesty, dominion and authority, **before all time** and now and forever. Amen."* (NAS)

At the instant of creation, time began. Prior to that, there was God!

Beginning (Hebrew - *reshith*); definition – beginning, chief; Strong's #7225
Before (Greek – *pro*); definition – before; Strong's #4253
Time (Greek – *aion*); definition – continued duration, a space of time, duration; Strong's #165

We are not talking about a space shuttle launch and the pre-launch countdown; T-5 and counting. Nope! God has always existed, He didn't

> **"Put your hand on a hot stove for a minute, and it seems like an hour. Sit with a pretty girl for an hour, and it seems like a minute. That's relativity" Einstein**

begin some time prior to the creation, He always was, the Eternal One. In grade school, we wrote timelines which had some beginning and identified or marked points of time on it. Our universe, the space-time-continuum that we live in, had a beginning and has been continuing ever since. But what about before that? It is referred to as "eternity past." Time is not a property of eternity and is therefore not counted. There is nothing to count.

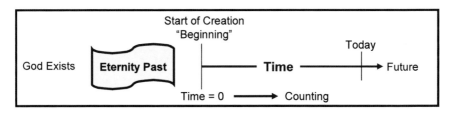

Scientists of the late 1800's and early 1900's insisted that the universe had existed "forever". We find today that this thought was in error. Cosmologists today (see examples below), who mostly follow one of the many "Big Bang" theories, all recognize that time began at the beginning of the "Big Bang". We find that the biblical text is in agreement with this concept, or perhaps better stated, the fact that time began at the beginning of creation was revealed in scriptures 3,500 years ago. Time Began at Creation; it is a difficult concept to grasp but time is a property of our physical universe (As noted by Einstein from his theories of relativity). Prior to the beginning of our space-time-continuum there was no time.

In his book, It's About Time, popular author and physicist Paul Davies remarks on the incredible discovery that time began at the beginning of the universe. "Modern scientific cosmology is the most ambitious enterprise of all to emerge from Einstein's work. When scientists began to explore the implications of Einstein's time for the universe as a whole, they made one of the most important discoveries in the history of human thought: that time, and hence all of physical reality, must have had a definite origin in the past. If time is flexible and mutable, as Einstein demonstrated, then it is possible for time to come into existence-and also to pass away again; there can be a beginning and an end to time." [30]

Physicist Tom Van Flandern on the subject of time; "The Big Bang theory is the accepted model for the origin of the universe. This theory requires us to accept the following: Time and Space have not always existed; both began a finite time ago; and both the age and size of the present universe are finite." [31]

1978 NASA astronomer Robert Jastrow, a self described agnostic – "I am fascinated by some strange developments going on in astronomy-partly

---

[30] "It's About Time"; Paul Davies; Touchstone Books/Simon and Schuster, 1995, pg. 17 as quoted in; http://www.khouse.org/articles/1999/233/
[31] "Dark Matter Missing Planets and New Comets"; Tom Van Flandern; North Atlantic Books; copyright 1993; revised edition; page XV

because of their religious implications and partly because of the peculiar reactions of my colleagues. The essence of the strange developments is that the universe had, in some sense, a beginning-that it began at a certain moment in time!" [32]

A closer examination of the first verse of scriptures:

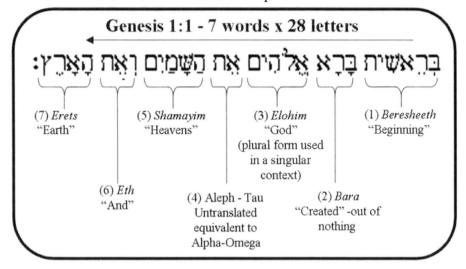

Genesis 1:1 - 7 words x 28 letters

בְּרֵאשִׁית בָּרָא אֱלֹהִים אֵת הַשָּׁמַיִם וְאֵת הָאָרֶץ:

(7) *Erets*
"Earth"

(6) *Eth*
"And"

(5) *Shamayim*
"Heavens"

(4) Aleph - Tau
Untranslated
equivalent to
Alpha-Omega

(3) *Elohim*
"God"
(plural form used
in a singular
context)

(2) *Bara*
"Created" -out of
nothing

(1) *Beresheeth*
"Beginning"

7 words x 28 letters [33] ; 7 being the number of spiritual perfection and 4 the number of creation [34] .

Further insights: The first word in scripture is "*Bershetes*" (sometimes written "*reshith*") – "in beginning." The first letter is shaped so as to indicate that what precedes this event is unknowable. "The first letter of the first word...is the Hebrew letter *beth* בּ . [Hebrew reads from right to left (not left to right as English) so the *beth* is at the right of the page and indicating a close to the right of it (before) and an open to the left (or after)]. It is on this seemingly irrelevant fact that the sages based their understanding that any knowledge of

---

[32] Answers to Atheists,
http://www.greatcom.org/resources/answers_for_atheists/ch_04/default.htm
[33] "Gleanings in Genesis – Vol I & II"; Arthur Pink; Moody Press; Copyright 1922; page 13
[34] "Number in Scripture"; E.W.Bullinger; Kregel Pub, 1967; re-print of original published in 1910; page 158 and page 123

what preceded the beginning is unattainable by investigation…because of the shape of *beth*." [35]

> # Eternity is not a lot of time.
> # It is an existence devoid of time.

For those who may feel that this is a bit contrived, I have some bad news. About 800 years ago, one of the three great Hebrew sages came to the same conclusion (without the benefit of understanding Einstein's relativity). Nachmanides noted in 1265 AD that time comes into being in the first verse of Genesis 1 and also from Genesis 1:5 noting that it was not "the first day"(which would have implied an already existing series) but it is more literally stated as "Day One" (implying the beginning of time). [36] (see also John 9:32). Maimonides, another Hebrew sage of the 11th century AD also wrote of time beginning in Genesis 1:1. [37]

> # Creator beyond time and space

---

[35] "Genesis and the Big Bang"; Gerald Schroeder, Ph.D.; Bantam Books; copyright 1990; page 56

[36] "Commentary on the Torah - Genesis"; Ramban Nachmanides; Translated by Rabbi Dr. Charles B. Chavel; Shilo Publishing House, NY; copyright 1999; page 32

[37] "Guide of the Perplexed" ; Maimonides; translated by M Friedlander; Hebrew Publishing Co.; Published 1901; Part II Chapter XIII Page 63; Maimonides, one of three great venerated Hebrew sages, wrote in the 11th century AD.

Isaiah 57:15
*"For thus saith the high and lofty One **that inhabiteth eternity**, whose name is Holy"* (emphasis author - KJV)

2 Timothy 1:8-9
*"...God, who has saved us and called us with a holy calling, not according to our works, but according to His own purpose and grace which was **given to us in Christ Jesus before time began**."* (emphasis author - NKJ)

Titus 1:2
*"...in hope of eternal life which God, who cannot lie, **promised before time began.**"* (emphasis author - NKJ)

Eph 2:10
*"For we are His workmanship, created in Christ Jesus for good works, which **God prepared beforehand**, that we should walk in them."* (emphasis author - NAS)

3 – General Physics

Chapter 3.2

Big Bang – Beginning of the Universe

Genesis 1:1 –
"*In the beginning God created the heavens and the earth.*" (NAS)

Jeremiah 10:12 See also Jeremiah 51:15
"*It is He who made the earth by His power, who established the world by His wisdom; and by His understanding **He has stretched out the heavens**.*" (emphasis author - NAS)

Hebrews 11:3
"*By faith we understand that the worlds were prepared by the word of God, so that **what is seen was not made out of things which are visible**.*" (emphasis author - NAS)

Isaiah 44:24 See also Isaiah 42:5; 45:5; 45:12; 51:13
"*I, the Lord, am the maker of all things, **stretching out the heavens** by Myself...*" (emphasis author)

Psalm 104:2
"*Covering Yourself with light as a cloak, **stretching out heaven like a tent curtain***" (emphasis author)

Creation Ex-Nihilo!

Created (Hebrew - *Bara*); definition – to shape or create (out of nothing); Strong's #1254
Formed (Greek – *yatsar*); definition – to form, fashion; Strong's #3335
Made (Greek – *asah*); definition – do, make; Strong's #6213a
Stretching (Hebrew – *natah*); definition – to stretch out, spread out, extend, incline, bend; Strong's #5186

3 – General Physics

"Now with this creation, which was like a very small point having no substance, everything in the heavens and on the earth was created." [38] That's a pretty good assessment of how, now in the 21st century, quantum physics views the beginning of the universe. However, shockingly, this statement was made by Ramban Nachmanides in 1265 AD. You read that right, about 800 years ago, Nachmanides, one of three of the most venerated Hebrew rabbis' viewed the creation as starting from a single point and expanding outward. For hundreds of years, this was viewed as a "quaint" thought. The advent of quantum physics and its subsequent development in the 20th century of various "Big Bang" theories have been developed that describe the

> **First there was nothing, then it exploded**

origin of the universe. Modern physicists and cosmologists typically ascribe to one of the "Big Bang" type concepts which, simply stated, describe the formation of the universe as starting from an extremely small point and bursting forth, expanding outward creating space and inaugurating the beginning of time. I like the way Chuck Missler states it; "First there was nothing, then it exploded!" [39]

Physicist Tom Flandern defines the Big Band Theory: "Big Bang Theory....all matter and energy in the entire universe was contained in an infinitesimal point at the 'beginning'; that for some unknown reason it all exploded...." [40]

There are three Hebrew words used to denote building or creating something. *Yatsa* (to form – like in Genesis 2:7 where God "formed" man from the dust of the ground); *Asa* (to make – like in Genesis 1:16 where God "made" two great lights (Sun and Moon)); and *Bara* (to create out of nothing). Genesis 1:1 uses *bara* with the declaration that it wasn't that something existed and from that, God made the universe. With wisdom and understanding that only God possesses, He created the universe, the time-space continuum that we now live in. As difficult as this is to grasp, it is important to note that matter didn't "explode" into a space that was there; there was no space. From a tiny spot, think of it as a seed, that contained all the particles of the universe (not atoms and molecules yet) packed together in a micro space, God begins to "stretch" out creating space as it progresses. The space-time- continuum is stretch out to

---

[38] "Ramban - Commentary on the Torah - Genesis"; Ramban Nachmanides – translated by Charles Chavel; Shilo Pub; copyright 1999; page 25
[39] "Book of Genesis – Comprehensive Workbook"; Dr. Chuck Missler; Koinonia House Pub; copyright 2004; page 30
[40] "Dark Matter, Missing Planets and New Comets"; Tom Van Flandern; North Atlantic Books; revised edition; copyright 1993; page 391

40

be now some billions of light years across. This is referred to as "Creation Ex Nihilo" or "from nothing." Scripturally, this is our understanding.

Curiously, we also know from Genesis 1 that the earth was not part of the basis creation of the universe. The earth appears in verse 2 and then on day 2, God begins to work with the earth. The earth was not a product of the big bang; (Ex 31:17) says "I made" using the *Asa* term.

Big Bang Cosmology

Most physicists today believe in some form of a big bang start to the universe. The basic premise is that the entire universe started at one point, at one instance in time. The theory today (suggested by Alan Guth), is the best one we have. Although still speculative, it states that the entire universe started from a single point of incredibly large mass but no space. It doesn't contain atoms; they haven't been formed yet, but particles. From the speck, an explosion started (growth), and when it was very small and very early in the growth (10^{-25} seconds and 10^{-24} centimeters in size), physicists today state that an outside force that is not in action today must have been exerted. Some type of anti-gravity force is postulated. The discussions continue today with people arguing about what happened after the 10^{-44} second after the "Bang" as they struggle to understand. The scientific implication the secular world struggles with, is that a creator is implied in this model. Isn't that interesting? "Big Bang" models have stemmed from the theories of relativity which provides the analytical basis. Specifically:

- Special Relativity – Einstein 1905; defines as $E=mc^2$
- General Relativity - Einstein 1915: No distinction between time and space: four-dimensional continuum;
  - o This theory has been confirmed 12 ways to 5 decimal places and is therefore becoming pretty solid
  - o Einstein's only real mistake which as later self-admitted was a cosmological constant, a "fudge factor" he included to formulate a static model in an initial attempt to deny the creative act demanded by the theory (a step he later regretted making)

From these analytical models, we find that the universe originated from a "singularity" (a point) and all 4 dimensions of space were compressed in zero size. Variations of the "Big Bang" models include:

- Steady State Models: initial models but these were refuted in the 1960's
- Hesitation Models: Same thing
- Oscillation Models: Refuted in 1984
- Inflation Models: These are currently in vogue:

- o Alan Guth states that MIR Forces are required in the initial phase of formation that are not observed today
- o This is viewed as a short term duration in either initial time or distance which is about 10^{-35} seconds = 10^{-24} centimeters.
- o Anti-gravity type of force is postulated.

Expanding Universe and Red Shift

Secular scientists generally assume that the universe is expanding due to the "red shift" seen in distant star measurements. Light from various stars have been measured with a shift towards the red color spectrum. A possible explanation for this is a "Doppler" type shift. A Doppler shift is a change in frequency due to velocity of travel away or towards the observer. An example is a car or train coming at you. You hear the noise of the approaching car in a higher pitch but right as it passes, what you hear shifts to a lower pitch or frequency. In a similar fashion, if a star is rapidly moving away from earth, we would expect to see a shifted light spectrum over stars who are not moving or moving away at a slower speed. Because of the extensive "red shift" of measured light from various stars, it has become the common belief that the universe is continuing to expand.

Assuming an "expansion" or biblically "stretching" of the creating process we are confronted with three options for the universe today:

- Continuing to Expand: common view based primarily on the "red shift" data
- Now static: the universe is neither contracting or expanding at the present time
- Contracting universe: the thought is that the universe expanded out like a rubber band with an explosion of energy, but now gravity would begin to pull things back together

Personally, I see that scriptures seem to indicate God "stretched" out the heavens, past tense. This indicates to me they are not in a continuing expansion process. Debates have continued within the physics community over the eventual death of the universe. Assuming no intervention from outside, it is now generally believed that the universe continuing to expand at an ever increasing rate. Renowned Physicist Dr. Kaku: "According to the picture emerging from the WMAP satellite, a mysterious antigravity force is accelerating the expansion of the universe."[41] Within the last 10 years, a few folks have begun to challenge the hypothesis that the "red shift" indicates an

---

[41] "Parallel Worlds", Michio Kaku, Doubleday, copyright 2005, Page 288

expanding universe. Recent measurements seem to indicate that the "red shift" is quantized or in specific steps. This means that an explosion should generate a full range of velocity values for the objects traveling away from the point of release (example: if we measured 5 objects we would expect to find their speeds randomly over the range (say if 1-15) something like 3,7,8,10 and 14. It should be a random sample. Instead what we find is discreet steeps like 5, 5, 10, 10, and 15; in this case, steps of 5. This suggests some other explanation rather than a Doppler causing velocity shift.

Foundation Rock of the Earth

There is also a curious Hebrew tradition, which states that this point, from which the universe was created, is referred to as "The rock of foundation" upon which the world was founded. This point also becomes the "foundation rock" upon which the Ark of the Covenant rested in the Holy of Holies." [42] It is thus believed by the ancient rabbis that the point of origin of the universe, becomes the "rock" of foundation for the earth. That foundational rock is located on Mt. Moriah, the location of the Jewish Temple, where the Ark of the Covenant once stood.

What about the Earth? – Gap Theory

 "Gap Theory". A concept of a "gap" of "time" between Genesis 1:1 and 1:2 has been debated for quite some time. KJV translated 2:1 as the "and the earth **was** without form and void." Nearly 200 years ago Dr. Chalmers [43] called attention to the fact that the word "was" should be translated "became." Some have speculated that in this gap can be found primitive man or dinosaurs. This is a clear contradiction with the subsequent passages primarily because no death existed prior to the fall of man (death having come by Adam – 1 Cor 15:27). However, one key piece of biblical evidence supporting a "gap" is the phrase "without form and void" or in the Hebrew, *Tohu W'bohu*. Genesis indicates that the earth became "*Tohu W'bohu*". Isaiah 45:18 speaking of the earth and creation states "He created it not in vain [*Tohu*]. Donald Grey Barnhouse developed the concept of a great spiritual catastrophe and indicates this is where Lucifer (the shinning one) becomes Satan (the adversary) in his book "The Invisible War". [44] This can become a lengthy in-depth study but my personal opinion is that it isn't worth the trip.

---

[42] "Commentary on the Torah - Genesis"; Ramban Nachmanides; page 26

[43] "Gleanings in Genesis – Vol I & II"; Arthur Pink; Moody Press; Copyright 1922; page 10

[44] "The Invisible War"; Donald Grey Barnhouse; Zondervan; copyright 1965; chapters 1-3

3 – General Physics

"And darkness was upon the face of the Abousso (deep)".

Chapter 3.3

Law of Decay – Bondage of Creation

Rom 8:19-21
*"For the anxious longing of the creation waits eagerly for the revealing of the sons of God. For the **creation was subjected to futility**, not of its own will, but because of Him who subjected it, in hope that the **creation itself also will be set free from its slavery to corruption** into the freedom of the glory of the children of God."* (NAS)

Corruption: (Greek *phthora*) definition: decay, ruin: Strong's #5356
Eagerly Waits: (Greek *apekdechomai*): "The verb for "eagerly waits" is used seven times in the New Testament, each time to refer to Christ's return (Rom 8:19, 23, 25; 1Cor 1:7; Gal 5:5; Phil 3:20; Heb 9:28). [45]

Gen 3:17-18
*"Then to Adam He said, "Because you have listened to the voice of your wife, and have eaten from the tree about which I commanded you, saying, 'You shall not eat from it'; **cursed is the ground because of you**; in toil you shall eat of it all the days of your life. "Both thorns and thistles it shall grow for you; and you shall eat the plants of the field;"* (NAS)

Entropy – Definition:

The 1st Law of Thermodynamics is the conservation of energy, which says that in any closed system, the total energy stays the same; energy can neither be created nor destroyed. The 2nd Laws states that entropy (randomness - chaos) can only increase. This is profound as it establishes the direction of time (we can only go forward) and it establishes the principle that heat flows from a hotter object to a cooler one.  Although this heat transfer is obvious, its implications

---

[45] "The Bible Knowledge Commentary – New Testament"; J. Walvoord & R. Zuck; Victor   Cook Communications; copyright 1983 & 2000; page 472

are subtler. Simply stated; (1) all hot objects are cooling down, (2) the universe must have had a beginning in which energy was infused and order created and (3) eventually the universe will run out of heat (energy). Left to its own, the universe will one-day "die" (referred to as "Heat Death"). Even though the Laws of Thermodynamics were defined less that 500 years ago, Psalm 129: 26, written over 3,000 years ago stated the same thing; "the heavens…will wear out like a garment."

Law	Stated	Description	C.P. Snow
1st Law	Conservation of Energy	Energy can neither be created or destroyed	You can't win
2nd Law	Law of Entropy (randomess)	Entropy (Randomess) can only increase	You can't break even
3rd Law	Absolute Zero Temperture	Entropy (Randomess) of a body at absolute zero is infinite	You can't even get out of the game

According to the 2nd law, all things experience increasing entropy (randomness) and eventually degrade, such as: [46]

- Signal   degraded by noise
- Information   degraded by error
- Design   degraded by chance
- Direction   degraded by random walk
- Order   degraded by chaos
- Music   degraded by cacophony
- Control   degraded by anarchy

All of science accepts and uses the 2nd Law except for the evolutionists. Evolution states that more order and information can come from "chance" which is completely contrary to the know law of Entropy.

How did all this get started? Energy was infused into creation from the beginning and is slowly being used up until one day when it will be all gone. Entropy (randomness – chaos) is increasing. When and how did the universe get "wound up?" This occurred during the 7 days of creation. The expression of "evening - *erev*" and "morning - *boker*" in Genesis 1 provide the insight.

---

[46] "The Book of Genesis"; Chuck Missler; Koinonia House Pub.; copyright 1995; supplemental notes – Chapters 1-2 - page 11

Chuck Missler: "The Hebrew terms, *erev*, and *boker*, now refer to "evening and "morning" but their origins remain obscure. *Erev* designates obscuration, mixture (increasing entropy). The time when encroaching darkness begins to deny the ability to discern forms, shapes, and identities; thus, it becomes a term for twilight or evening. This also marks the duration of impurity, when a ceremonially unclean person became clean again, and thus, the beginning of the Hebrew day.

"*Boker* is a designation for becoming discernible, distinguishable, visible; perception of order; relief of obscurity (decreasing entropy). It thus is associated with being able to begin to discern forms, shapes, and distinct identities; breaking forth of light; revealing; hence, denotatively, dawn, morning. (As traditional designations for the Hebrew day, technically it would  seem to only designate the night-time hours, but it is used connotatively for the entire calendar day.) [47]

In each of the 6 creation days, God added information and energy, decreasing entropy. Secular scientists recognize that entropy (chaos) was low at the beginning. "Perfect order in the Universe occurred the instance after the Big Bang when energy and matter and all of the **forces of the Universe were unified**." [48] Even though this fact was only discovered through modern science, we find that once again, this insight was revealed over 3,500 years ago through Moses.

Genesis 1:31 "*And God saw all that He had made, and behold, it was very good.*" Recognizing the series and progression of "it was good" and seeing the 6th day "very good," Onkelos (a premier Hebrew scholar of the 3rd century) translated Gen 1:31 as "**and it was a unified order**" over 1,800 years ago. [49]

---

[47] Chuck Missler; "Why Six Days"; Article in "Personal Update"; Volume 13, No 11; November 2003; page 13

[48] http://www.physicalgeography.net/fundamentals/6e.html

[49] "Genesis and the Big Bang"; Gerald Schroeder; Bantam Books; copyright 1990; page 103

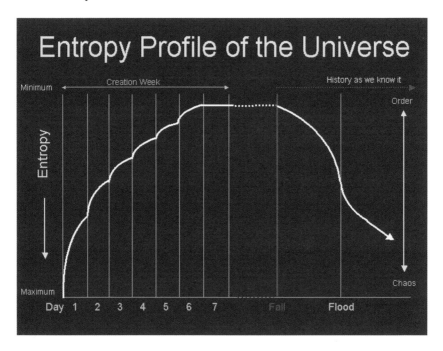

Entropy decreased over the 6 days of creation as God "wound up" the Universe [50]

Creation is Temporarily Subject to Decay (Entropy)

If order was increased on each of the 6 days of the creation, when did the direction reverse and entropy (chaos) begin to increase? There are two primary thoughts on this: Some feel that it was on the 7th day, when God rested from His creating, no longer adding energy and information and a few link it to the fall of Adam in Genesis 3.

7th Day thoughts:

Henry Morris: "But during the period of Creation, God was introducing order and organization and energization into the universe in a very high degree, even to life itself! It is thus quite plain that the processes used by God in creation were utterly different from the processes, which now operate in the universe! The creation was a unique period, entirely incommensurate with this present world." [51]

---

[50] Chart from Dr. Chuck Missler – Koinonia House:
http://www.khouse.org/articles/2001/361/
[51] "The Genesis Flood"; John C. Whitcomb and Henry Morris; Presbyterian and Reformed Publishing Company; copyright 1961; 42nd printing, February 1998, page 223

Maimonides (12th century Hebrew Sage): "that is to say, while on each of the six days events took place contrary to the natural laws now in operation, throughout the Universe, on the seventh day the Universe was merely upheld and left in the condition in which it continues to exist." [52]

Thoughts from the fall:

Some of us see that Adam and Eve were living in this perfect world, and even though I would imagine that heat flowed from hot objects to cooler objects, the general law of decay (entropy) was not increasing until the curse was placed on man and the earth which occurred at the "fall of Man" in the Garden of Eden. In was in Genesis 3:17-18 that we saw the ground (earth) being cursed. Death comes on to the scene according to Romans 5:14 "*Nevertheless **death reigned from Adam** until Moses, even over those who had not sinned in the likeness of the offense of Adam, who is a type of Him who was to come.*" (NAS)

Chuck Missler: "In the beginning there apparently was a close connection between the spiritual and physical realms, until the fall of man in Genesis 3. The universe was pronounced "good" - - free of defects - - by the Creator. A high degree of order originally existed; that is, there was very low entropy. But then Adam fell and the curse of sin began. Disorder and entropy began to increase...The subsequent death, dying, decaying, and destroying process affected not only man, but nature as well (Rom 8:19-23." [53]

Life in Eden was great, we find Adam walking and talking with God. I don't think we can even begin to comprehend what life was like at that time, it must have been completely different than it is today. I see the 2nd Law of Thermodynamics being instituted at the fall, at the curse.

Will the Universe Always be Cursed?

Gratefully not! Revelation tells us of the New Heavens and New Earth that will come after the Millennium (or the 1,000-year reign of Christ on earth) will be completely different from our earth of today.

---

[52] "Guide of the Perplexed - Part I - Maimonides" ; Translated by M. Friedlander; Hebrew Publishing Co. New York; first Published 1901; page 251
[53] Notes from "Genesis and the Big Bang"; audio commentary on Genesis by Chuck Missler; page 10

3 – General Physics

Rev 21:4-6 *"...and He shall wipe away every tear from their eyes; **_and there shall no longer be any death;_** there shall no longer be any mourning, or crying, or pain; the first things have passed away." And He who sits on the throne said, "Behold, I am making all things new." And He said, "Write, for these words are faithful and true." And He said to me, "It is done. I am the Alpha and the Omega, the beginning and the end. I will give to the one who thirsts from the spring of the water of life without cost."* (NAS)

> **"The Lord, who has heard the tears of the believers, has also heard the groaning of His creation. Its cries shall be stilled and it will lie in peace."**

Donald Grey Barnhouse [54]

Creation will be set free to be what God intended. We will live in our "resurrected bodies" (hyperspace). And, there will be no more death, or mourning, or crying, or pain; the old things have passed away. I believe the 2nd Law of Thermodynamics, the Law of Entropy, will be repealed and thrown out.

---

[54] "Romans – Vol III"; Donald Grey Barnhouse; Eerdmans Pub; copyright 1963; God's Heirs - Chapter VI - page 129

Chapter 3.4

Light and the Message of Jesus

Job 38:19
*"**Where is the way to the dwelling of light**? And darkness, where is its place,"* (NAS)

Where does light come from? No one knows!

Dwelling: (Hebrew – *shakan*) definition: to reside, dwell, abide, to let oneself down, to settle down – Strong's # 7931

Light: (Hebrew – *ore* – Greek – *phos*) definition: illumination or illuminary – Strong's # 216

Scientifically, one of the most challenging verses in the Bible. Job, the oldest book in the Bible, contains a challenge. A challenge put forth by God to Job. After several chapters of Job and his friends arguing and debating about what was really going on and what they knew, God breathes into the last chapters amazing revelations and unbelievable scientific insights, some that still puzzle us today.   If ever you think you are really beginning to understand and know things; read Job 37-39 and be very, very humbled.

[55]

- For nearly one hundred years, debates raged as to whether light was an electromagnetic wave or if it was a particle

> **186,000 Miles Per Second**
> **It's Not Just a Good Idea,**
> **It's The Law !**

- In 1906, J. J. Thomson was awarded the Nobel Prize for his work proving that electrons were particles
- 31 years later, in 1937 J. J. Thomson saw his son George Thomson receive the Nobel Prize for his work proving that electrons were waves (as a co-award winner).
- Scientific understanding today refers to the "Duality of Light." Light consists of both an electromagnetic wave and at the same time, is a particle (named the photon).

---

[55] Quote in the box making reference to the speed of light is found humorous by physic techies.

What is a wave? A wave does not contain matter in itself. Like the wave on the surface of the ocean or that created by throwing a rock in a pond. Electromagnetic waves are similar. A radio wave is also an electromagnetic wave, traveling through air. Energizing something can generate waves, in essence, by making it "vibrate." OK, but what about the particles. If light is a photon, where are the photons living just before the light is sent out. Well, that's the trick. In my attempt to understand this after reading Job 38 (where does light dwell) I had a detailed discussion with a friend, Neil Tornberg at work who is a Christian and a PHD physicist. He is a really smart person who has a good understanding of physics and electromagnetic waves. We had a lengthy discussion but I felt I wasn't getting my question answered. Does a light bulb have a bunch of photons that get released when electricity is applied? Apparently not! Where is a photon before it was emitted? It was beginning to sound like it didn't exist before all of a sudden, it was flying through space. Towards the end of the conversation, in frustration Neil finally exclaimed "it is much easier to understand the Trinity than it is to understand where the photons come from!!!" Well, there we have it. Since no one really understands or can explain the Trinity, although we know it is real, I figured it would be some time before I mastered the problem of "where light lived." [56]

> **Fun Fact:**
> The total amount of electrical activity going on in your brain amounts to only about one-hundredths of a watt, which means it would take a thousand people's brains to light a 20-wat bulb.

---

[56] It is my personal opinion that one day we may discover that there are 3 parts to light. This comes from the thought that "God is light" and yet there is Father, Son and Spirit, 3 parts, not just two.

Stunning Biblical revelations concerning Light

Light Itself
- The first recorded spoken words of God are: "Let there be light" or more precisely "Let light be" (Genesis 1:3)
- God **made** everything except light. Light, He just commanded into existence (Genesis 1) [57]
- God is still "forming" the light. He is active in the process; *"The One **forming light** and creating darkness, causing well-being and creating calamity; I am the LORD who does all these."* Isa 45:7 (NAS) [58]
- Light was the first to appear in the 7 days of creation. (Gen 1)
- Light is *phos* in the Greek – it is used 72 times in scripture (3^2 x 6) [59]
- Music is waves of a frequency that our ears are tuned to, so we can hear. If light is waves, it is music but we just don't hear it. [60] (from physics)
- The Sun's light is the source of all energy on earth (from physics)

God and light
- Jesus came to this earth to do many things, but what most people don't realize is that He brought a

> **Light is declared by the Scriptures to have come into existence by the express decree of the Almighty and to have been in existence long before man or animals or vegetables had their being"** [61]

message. If Jesus came to earth to bring us this message, what is it? Why don't we all recognize the most important thing Jesus said? Actually it is a simple but deeply profound message. Listen carefully: *"And this is the message we have heard from Him and announce to you, **that God is light, and in Him there is no darkness at all**."* I John 1:5 NAS Wow!!! Meditate on that for a while!

---

[57] "God's Living Oracles"; Arthur Pierson; Pickering & Inglis Pub; copyright 1904; page 49

[58] Note in this verse that darkness is not the absence of light. God is "creating darkness" – creating is the Hebrew word *bara* (Strong's #1254) meaning creating "out of nothing." – Genesis 1:1 "In the beginning God created [*bara* – out of nothing] the heavens and the earth."

[59] "Numbers in Scripture"; E.W. Bullinger; Kregel Pub; first published 1897; reprint pub 1967; page 28 [includes Eph 5:9 and Rev 22:5]

[60] Ibid.; page 56

[61] "New Unger's Bible Dictionary"; originally published by Moody Press of Chicago, Ill. Copyright 1988 – electronic version *Light*

- God dwells in unapproachable light (1 Tim 6:16) *"who alone possesses immortality and __dwells in unapproachable light__; whom no man has seen or can see. To Him be honor and eternal dominion! Amen."* (NAS) [62]

Jesus and Light

- John 1:9 *__"[Jesus] was the true light__ which, coming into the world, enlightens every man."* (NAS)
- John 8:12 *"Again therefore Jesus spoke to them, saying, "__I am the light of the world__; he who follows Me shall not walk in the darkness, but shall have the light of life."* (NAS)
- John 1:4-5 *"In Him [Jesus] was life, and the life was the __light of men__. And the light shines in the darkness, and the darkness did not comprehend it."* (NAS)
- Acts 26:23 *"that the Christ was to suffer, and that by __reason of His resurrection from the dead He should be the first to proclaim light__ both to the Jewish people and to the Gentiles."* (NAS)
- Darkness fell upon the land for 3 hours as Jesus was crucified (Matt 27:45)

> **The important Message of Jesus:**
> "God is light, and in Him there is no darkness at all"

Christians:

- We are to walk as "Children of the Light"; Ephesians 5:8 *"for you were formerly darkness, but now you are light in the Lord; __walk as children of light__"* (NAS)
- We receive and inheritance from God as "Saints in Light" (Colossians 1:12)
- NIV translates the Kingdom to "Kingdom of Light" - Col 1:12 *"giving thanks to the Father, who has qualified you to share in the inheritance of the saints in the __kingdom of light__."* (NIV)
- We put on the "Armor of Light"; Romans 13:12-14 *"The night is almost gone, and the day is at hand. Let us therefore lay aside the deeds of darkness and __put on the armor of light__...put on the Lord Jesus Christ"* (NAS)

---

[62] It is an often-overlooked subtlety that only God is immortal. We can have everlasting life but we had a beginning. God had neither beginning nor an end, He is from eternity past through eternity future.

- The story of Gideon (Judges 6 & 7) contains a subtle "type" for us to learn. Gideon with a small band of 300 God selected soldiers, overcame the forces of a mighty army over 100 times their size by setting up a perimeter at night around the enemy camp. All they did was to break clay pots that had lights in them and sound horns. In the confusion of darkness, the enemy attacked themselves and completely self-destructed. In the "type" we, as the "light bears" for Christ when we become broken of our own strength, and allow the Light of Christ to shine out of us, miraculous things happen.
- The eye is the lamp [light] of the body: Matt 6:22 "***The lamp of the body is the eye***; *if therefore your eye is clear, your whole body will be full of light.*" (NAS)
- We are called out of darkness into His marvelous light (1 Peter 2:9)

> "And in the beginning there was nothing. And God said "Let there be light." And there was still nothing but now you could see it"
> Anonymous [63]

Can we "see" God?

Moses wanted to "see" God's glory (Exodus 33:18-23) but was told that he could not see God's face because "no man can see Me and live." Instead, Moses was instructed to hide in a special place in a cleft of a rock and God would pass by. As God passed by, He covered the place where Moses could see out with His hand, once past, Moses was allowed to see God's back. Moses also, because of his time with God, had his face begin to radiate (glow). He wears a veil over his face as he meets with the Israelites to prevent them from seeing this "glory."

In Revelation 1:16, John gets to see a vision of Jesus in heaven and His "face was like the sun shinning in its strength." I find this fascinating that when we see Jesus in His glory (or radiance), His face is like starring into the sun. It is something we are incapable of doing, we are not designed to look directly into the sun. However, according to 2 Corinthians 3:18, before we come to God, we also can not see (as to fully understand) God because there is a "veil" over out hearts. When we come to God, the veil is lifted, allowing us to see and understand, giving us liberty. This is somewhat limited, for we see "as in a

---

[63] The unusually quote was found in; "Dark Matter, Missing Planets & New Comets"; Tom Van Flandern; North Atlantic Books; copyright 1993; revised edition; page 393

mirror" but one day when we receive our newly resurrected bodies, we will see Him as He is, because we will be like Him." (1 John 3:2)

Moses, because even though he was an obedient follower of God, still had sin in him and could not look upon God. Now that Christ has died for our sins, we are made new (if we have repented and asked Christ to be our Lord and Savior), a new creation, and all our sins are cleansed from us. In this condition, we can not only look upon Jesus, but are instructed to do so.

I remember watching some experiments where some scientists were focusing extremely high power, very intense light into plastic fiber optic lines. If there was any particle of dirt, any imperfection, the light would be absorbed by that imperfection and begin to get hot. As it got hot, the area would begin to burn and char. This would cause a lot more light to be absorbed by the now growing imperfection and a run-away condition quickly began to form leading to complete melt down. If, however, the connection to the fiber optic line was pure and clean, light would be able to travel through the interface without resulting in any heat being generated. If the interface contained no defects, high intense light could be passed through for an indefinite length of time. If we have been cleansed of all our sins, we can come into the presence of God and not be burned by the intensity of His radiant Glory. We can look full into His face. Heb 4:16a: *"Let us therefore come boldly unto the throne of grace..."*

Conjecture – Clothing of "Light" [64]

In Genesis 3:7 after Adam and Eve sinned by eating from the forbidden tree, we find that they "Knew they were naked." Most folks assume that the innocence of Adam and Eve allowed them to run around naked and not be ashamed. This however appears to conflict with other biblical facts. I think something else is going on here. As a result of Adam and Eve's fall, all of creation became cursed and I think this had a far reaching impact that we only see the result of and are only left to speculate what creation was like before the fall. It is my opinion that Adam and Eve had a "covering" that was lost in the fall and their nakedness was exposed. This rational is supported by the following observations:

♦ God does not desire to look upon our nakedness (Ex 20:26 example) and if Adam and Eve were naked, it would be contradictory as the Lord walked with them in the garden.

♦ In heaven, we will all be in robes of "white" (Rev 7:9)

---

[64] This conjecture is not my own thought but one that I heard from Dr. Chuck Missler.

♦ Angels often appear as "bright" or "shinning" (Luke 2:9)
♦ It is my opinion the angels and Adam at one time, have clothes of "light" and the glory of them covers the body. When Adam sinned, he lost the covering of "glory."

3 – General Physics

Chapter 3.5

Word of God is Active

Heb 4:12
"*For the __word of God is living and active__ and sharper than any two-edged sword, and piercing as far as the division of soul and spirit, of both joints and marrow, and able to judge the thoughts and intentions of the heart.*" (NAS)

Active: (Greek - *energēs*) definition: at work, active; Strong's #1756

Engineering Active

I am fascinated by the word "active" as it is applied to the "Word of God." For several years, I managed an engineering group called "active-adaptive." To an engineer, active means dynamic, bodies in motion, doing something. Active is contrasted against "passive."

Active	Passive
Car on the freeway	Car in the junkyard
Heating and Air conditioning System	Rock
Interactive computer game	Dice
Chameleon Skin	Shed snake skin
Word of God	Boy Scout Manual

Active Word

"The Word of God is alive, actively alive, and as the tense of the word indicates, constantly active. It is powerful. The word "powerful" ["Active in the NAS] is the translation of *energes* from which we get our word "energy," and which means "active, energizing.""" [65]

---

[65] "Word Studies in the New Testament – Vol II"; Kenneth Wuest; Eerdmans Pub; copyright 1947; reprint 2002; Hebrews - page 88

3 – General Physics

Active and Living; Is the bible a manual that we can read and determine direction and principles for our lives? Yes, but that thought falls way short of the value and worth of the Words of God as recorded in the bible. True, to begin with, these are the actual words of God as the Hebrew writer reminded us in chapter 1 verse 1; "in times past, God spoke…" It is God speaking, and God does not lie (Numbers 23:19). God speaks with clarity and purpose, and it is not by interpretation (2 Peter 1:20) that we understand the scriptures, it is by the leading of the Holy Spirit. Because this is God speaking, the words also transcend time. Much more that a recording of history or statements of doctrinal beliefs, it is God speaking. When I read the bible every morning, it is God speaking to me. He speaks to me, personally, on that day, for that day. The fact that the bible is active separates it from any other book ever written. It is the only book that is in essence, interactive. There have been many days when I have needed encouragement and God has spoken encouragement through the bible. There have been days when I have sought direction from the Lord, and He has provided that direction from the reading of the scriptures. My suggestion to you is this. When you pick up the bible to read it every day, before you start, ask God to help you understand what He wants to say to you today. After you read ask yourself, "God why did you tell me that today? What does that mean for me today?" Let God speak to you. Isn't it fantastic that God Himself meets with us as we read. We can hear His voice speaking directly to us everyday.

Pony Express riders who traveled through dangerous Indian country of the old American West used the lightest saddles and a very flat leather bag to hold the mail. To cut down weight they carried no rifles and the mail they carried was written on very thin paper. Postage rate was $5.00 per ounce (equal to $200 per letter in today's currency). Despite this, the managers of the Pony Express presented to every rider when they signed on, a special full size Pony Express Bible that they carried as part of their regular gear

An important facet for our moving forward in our relationship with God, is the fact that the Word of God is the answer to the problem of unbelief of the preceding passages. This is beautifully illustrated in Romans 10:17 *"So faith comes from hearing, and hearing by the word of Christ."* (NAS) The answer to un-belief is the Word of God. The more we read, the more we understand about God, and it causes our faith to grow. I read Hebrews Chapter 11 more than any other chapter in the Bible because it encourages me when I read about those who have, in faith, gone before me. My faith grows when I read about how God works in people's lives and meets their needs. How God loves us and takes care of us in difficult and trying times. My relationship with God grows and is strengthened as I learn more and more about Him.

Fun Facts:

Oldest Biblical Inscription

In the Israel Museum is a necklace charm, which is a rolled thin piece of pure silver. It has been dated to over 2,700 years ago, seven centuries before Christ and four hundred years before the writings of most of the Dead Sea Scrolls. Inscribe on it is the blessing that God gave the nation of Israel; Num 6:24-26 *"' "The LORD bless you and keep you; the LORD make his face shine upon you and be gracious to you; the LORD turn his face toward you and give you peace." '*

Sir Walter Scott, author of over sixty popular books asked on this deathbed for "the book" from his huge library, and when questioned he said, "There is only one book" pointing to the Bible.

Abraham Lincoln wrote, " I believe that the Bible is the best gift God has ever given to man. All the good from the Savior of the world is communicated to us through the book."

Henry M Stanley a brilliant explorer left on his trek to find the missionary Dr. David Livingstone in deep Africa with considerable gear including 180 pounds of books. When he found Livingstone the doctor talked of conversion of many cannibalistic tribes in Africa to Christianity. Stanley reported after his return that all the books were burned for fuel in fires except his Bible in which he stated he had read from Genesis to Revelation three times during his journey.

The **original Puritan settlers** who landed on Plymouth Rock laid a foundation of educational system dedicated to training "a learned clergy and a lettered people". Within a generation of landing, they founded "Harvard College in 1636 as a Christian college dedicated to upholding the truths of the Bible and established the school charter as; "Everyone shall consider the main end of his life and studies to know Jesus Christ which is eternal life."

3 – General Physics

<u>**Attempts to eliminate the Bible**</u> have failed including Roman Emperor Diocletian who in AD. 303 issued an official decree to kill all Christians and burn their sacred book.

> **The New Testament is the most widely quoted book in history.**

President Andrew Jackson on his deathbed pointed to the Bible next to him and stated "That Book, Sir, is the rock on which our Republic rests."

An African prince's ambassador questioned <u>**Queen Victoria**</u>, the greatest queen of England what the secret of the country's power and success throughout the world. The Queen picked up her Bible and said "Tell your prince that this book is the secret of England's greatness."

Napoleon: "The Bible is no mere book, but it is a living creature, with a power that conquers all that oppose it." [66]

<u>**Jesus**</u>, who at one of the greatest times of trial and at a point of weakness, was tempted by Satan himself. Jesus responded by quoting the Bible three times.

---

[66] "Learn the Bible in 24 hours"; Dr. Chuck Missler; Koinonia House Pub; copyright 2005; page 6

Chapter 3.6

Twinkle of an Eye

1 Corinthians 15:51-53
"Behold, I tell you a mystery; we will not all sleep, but we will all be changed, **in a moment**, in the **twinkling of an eye**, at the last trumpet; for the trumpet will sound, and the dead will be raised imperishable, and **we will be changed**. For this perishable must put on the imperishable, and this mortal must put on immortality." (NAS)

Moment (Greek: *atomos*) Definition: that can not be cut in two or divided, indivisible: Strong's #823
Twinkling: (*rhipē*) Definition: a throw, stroke or beat; Strong's #4493 (used only once in scripture)
Changed: (Greek: *allasso*) Definition; meaning; to change, to exchange one thing for another, to transform; Strong's 236 (used 6x)

"Faster than a speeding bullet"

This is a provocative passage giving a reference to time. The subject is the "rapture" of the Church (see 1 Thess 4:13-18) which is where believers in Christ that are alive on earth are instantly resurrected without going through the natural process of death. As fascinating as this event is, what I want to focus on here is the speed of transformation. All believers will one day be transformed from an natural, earthly body into a multi-dimensional, resurrected body (as prototyped by Jesus in His post resurrection appearances). We go from "mortal" to "immortality." Looking forward to that, but what is impressive is the speed.

Two words or phrases are used to describe the duration of time it will take to transform. First is the word "moment." Moment is a translation of the Greek *atomos* which is where we get our English word "atom." An atom is the smallest unit or size that a material can be broken into an still be that same

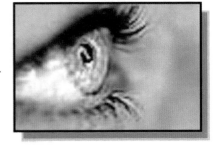

material. Any further breakdown results in protons, electrons and neutrons which are the same for all matter. So, *atomos* (moment) gives us the connotation of the smallest unit of time. *Atomos* means: that can not be cut in two or indivisible. In essence, the smallest possible increment of time possible.

A "twinkle of the eye" is not to be confused with a blink (which is about 1/100 of a second). A twinkle is defined as flickering or gleam of light. We are talking light speed. In the scriptural text, the word twinkle is from the Greek *rhipē* (used only once in the entire scripture) and means a throw, stroke or beat. *Rhipē* comes from the root word *rhipto* meaning; to cast, throw, or throw down.

Textual Insight:
Basically the text is telling us that in the smallest increment of time possible; we will be changed, exchanging our old natural bodies (casting them aside – throwing them down) for our new hyperspace bodies. Fantastic! We find nothing else in scripture stated to happen or be as quick as the transformation into hyperspace bodies at the time of the Rapture.

Scientific Insight:
It is initially shocking to find that time is only divisible into a minimum increment. Our normal tendency is to think that if something can be divided into a small part "A." Why can't we cut it in half and make a ½ part "A"? Turns out that quantum physics and string theory has given us the shocking discovery that the dimensions of the universe have a minimum size (known as the "Planck length" – 10^{-35} meters) and a minimum increment of time, known as the  "Planck time." Planck time is defined as the time it takes light, traveling at the speed of light, to go one Planck Length which turns out to be about 10^{-43} seconds, pretty fast.

Although we have only known for a few years that time is quantized, or unitized which means that there is a smallest increment of time possible, the biblical text seems to anticipate this although written nearly 2,000 years ago.

Chapter 4.1

Cycle of Water Including Rain, Rivers and Oceans

Job 36:27-28; see also Eccl 11:3; Job 26:8; Amos 9:6 Psalm 135:7; Jer 10:13; Isa 55:10; Job 37:11

"*For He **draws up the drops of water, they distill rain from the mist, which the clouds pour down**, they drip upon man abundantly.*" (NAS)

Eccl 1:7
"*All the rivers flow into the sea, yet the sea is not full. To the place where the rivers flow, there they flow again.*" (NAS)

Renewable water supply for man and living things

What is the source of water for the clouds?
Why isn't the ocean rising from the flow of rivers?

For centuries, people have struggled to understand where the rainwater has come from and the impact of constantly flowing rivers into the ocean. Clouds just appear and rain eventually follows (unless you live in the Arizona desert like I do where rarely do clouds form

> **Fun Facts:**
> • For every gallon of water in the ocean,
>   • There is a half of cup of water in the rivers, lakes and ground water
>   • There is almost two drops of water in the atmosphere
> • For every person, every minute; 44 gallons of rain water fall onto the earth

and even rarer does rain fall). Independent studies by two Frenchmen (yes, we have to give the French credit) led to the foundation of what is now called the "Hydrocycle" of the earth. Pierre Perrault (1608-1680) published in 1674; "On the Origin of Springs" based on his work studying rain and the Seine River. Edmond Marriotte (1620-1684) did similar work and they demonstrated that the rain and snowfall was sufficient to support the Seine River flow. Even though this foundational work was done in the 17th century, we find that the scriptures have clearly described the process and yet were written around 1500 BC. Job, which is considered the oldest of the biblical writings (other than the first 7 chapters of Genisis) clearly describes the Hydrocycle process. King Solomon, who was perhaps the wisest person ever on earth also gives us a brief description in Ecclesiastes. Was it Job's wisdom that allowed him to pen the water cycle even though it is not obvious to the observer or was it one of the many insights recorded in Job that are most certainly divine insights?

What is the Water Cycle?

Simply stated, ocean water is heated by the sun and causing evaporation of the water (without the salts and minerals in the water) which rises into the atmosphere. As atmospheric conditions permit due to cooler air at higher altitudes, the water condenses or condenses and freezes and forming extreemly fine droplets which make up the clouds. Clouds are formed either over the ocean or over the land and travel with the earth's wind currents (see next section 4.2). As conditions change, the clouds release their water and/or ice/snow which falls to the ground filling the rivers, lakes and replenishing underground water supplies. This water either flows back into the ocean or is evaporated back into the atmosphere. See figure for details.

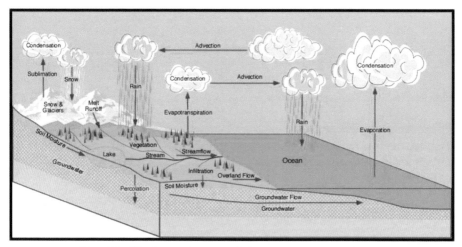

Earth's Hydrocycle describing the Water's Cycle

Man has been very dependent on rain to support the growth of crops. God, in His justice and mercy has used the abundance or withholding of rain as He stirs and tests the hearts of man. The first appearance of rain on the earth is at the Flood of Noah and it is used in judgment. Abraham experienced several famines presumably brought on by drought and God told the Israelites that He would both give them rain as a blessing (Deut 11:14; Heb 6:7-9) and withold it if they were sinful for the purpose of turning their hearts back to Him (Deut 11:17; 1 Kings 8:35-36; Amos 4:7). Jesus made a very revealing statement that rain is an illustration of how we are to love others. Matt 5:45-46 states:

Matt 5:45-46

"In order that you may be sons of your Father who is in heaven; for He causes His sun to rise on the evil and the good, and sends rain on the righteous and the unrighteous. For if you love those who love you, what reward have you? Do not even the tax-gatherers do the same?" (NAS)

Both the righteous and unrighteous receive the blessing of rain, and so to should we love not only those who love us but those who despise us. Challenging!!

4 – Earth Sciences

Chapter 4.2

Paths of the Sea

Matthew Maury's belief in the scientific accuracy of the scriptures was so great that he devoted years of his life doing extensive research on that assumption alone. The published results of this work revolutionized global navigation of the shipping industry resulting in Maury receiving highest honors from virtually every shipping country on the planet. All of this from one simple phrase in one simple verse of the bible.

Verses
Psalm 8:8 *"The birds of the air, and the fish of the sea that pass through the **paths of the seas**."* (NKJ)

Eccl 1:6 *"The wind blows to the south and turns to the north; **round and round it goes, ever returning on its course**."* (NIV)

Overview
If we listen, we can hear God speaking. If we are quiet and open, He whispers truth, wisdom and knowledge. God's speech is not limited to "how to live your life" or "what does this mean?" It can include new, shocking and completely astounding scientific information. On very special occasions, God reveals truths not previously understood but of such importance that the entire world becomes impacted. Because these truths can be sublime or run counter culture to the current thinking of the time faith is required. Great faith is required to accept and act on something simply

because it is declared to be so in the bible but yet goes against normal thinking. But it is to those with great faith that God on rare occasions provides a very precious and exquisite gem of new scientific truth. Matthew Fontaine Maury was a man of great faith in the God of the bible and it was to him that God chose to highlight a scientific truth that would eventually make a dramatic impact on the world of his time and leave a lasting legacy in Naval history.

Maury (1806-1873) was an officer in the United States Navy and had spent many years on the seas aboard the sailing ships of the time. One day, while recovering from sickness, Maury was home in bed and had requested that his son read to him from the bible. In the course of the reading, his son read Psalm 8:8, which makes an interesting, reference to "the paths of the sea." At this time, no one had considered that there were "paths" for the sea or winds. They were mostly thought to be random and chaotic in nature. "Maury had him [his son] read it over several times. Finally he said, 'If God says there are paths in the sea I am going to find them if I get out of this bed.'" [67] Acting with great faith, Maury decided to accept this proposition and spent the next several years working with the logs of many ships and taking measurements at sea in an attempt to identify the "paths." God honored Maury's faith and in 1854 he published a book identifying the ocean and wind currents that revolutionized the shipping industry and world economy of the time and still it serves as the basis of the ocean navigation today.

> **"There is no more worthy or suitable employment of the human mind than to trace the evidences of design and purpose in the Creator, which are visible in many parts of the creation" M. Maury** [68]

What did Maury Discover?

Ocean currents and wind currents are well known today, but they were unknown in Maury's time. Sea travel was the mode of transportation of the day and trips were often long and arduous because the sailing vessels were subject to the mercy of the winds and ocean currents. Shipping from Europe to America or from the American eastern seaboard round the Cape of Hope to America's western seaboard were laboriously long and associated costs drove the prices of the goods thus shipped. Sailing vessels were often sailing over ocean currents going in the opposite direction and bucking head winds as they crossed the oceans. Acting on the revelation from God that there were "Paths in the sea", he conducted extensive lab and field research. He was eventually

---

[67] "Matthew Fontaine Maury"; Charles Lewis; United States Naval Institute; published 1927; page 252

[68] "The Physical Geography of the Sea"; M.F. Maury; Harper and Brothers Pub; 3rd edition; 1855; page 68

able to identify both the sea and wind currents (paths) and published them in a book, "The Physical Geography of the Sea" in 1855. Included are descriptive texts as well as charts and plates of the wind and ocean currents. Maury successfully charted all the major ocean currents, the wind currents around the globe and other key oceanographic data including plotting the ocean depth from Europe to the Americas. The book had an immediate impact on world economy.

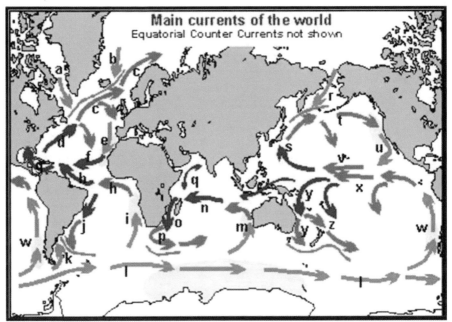

Ocean Currents of the Earth

Impact of Maury's Discover?

The global shipping industry immediately took advantage of this astounding research. Travel time between major ports began to drastically reduce. As an example, the average passage from New York to San Francisco was typically 180 days, or 6 months. Using Maury's charts that travel time was cut to 133 days and shortly thereafter to less that 110 days. That is two months off a 6-month trip or a 1/3 reduction. [69] The impact on the shipping nations of the time was so great that Maury received the highest honors countries could bestow on civilians. In addition to multiple honors in the United States, Maury was made a knight of the Order of Dannebrog by the King of Denmark (1856), knighted

---

[69] "Matthew Fontaine Maury"; Charles Lewis; United States Naval Institute; published 1927; page 60

by the Order of St. Anne by the Czar of Russia (1857), was made a commander of the Legion of Honor by the Emperor of France (1857) and was conferred the Order of the Tower and Sword by the King of Portugal (1859) all in addition to gold medals from Norway, Sweden, Prussia and the Republic of Bremen, Holland, Austria, Sardinia and France and others. [70]

Maury is broadly known today as the "Path finder of the Sea", [71] and is considered as the "Father of Modern Oceanography" and is highly honored at both the Naval Observatory and United States Naval Academy.

Wind Currents of Earth

Maury's Faith in God and The Scriptures

It was Maury's deep faith in the bible that enabled him to make such a significant scientific contribution to the world at large. Maury recognized that if the bible were the "Words of God", they must be accurate in all senses including scientific. It is based on the assumption that "God can not lie" making scripture complete truth. Maury himself says it best giving guidance to all those who work in the scientific field:

"The Bible frequently makes allusions to the laws of nature, their operation and effects. But such allusions are often so wrapped in the folds of the peculiar and graceful drapery with which its language is occasionally clothed, that the meaning, though peeping out from its thin covering all the while, yet lies in some sense concealed, until the lights and revelations of science are thrown upon it; then it bursts out and strikes us with the more force and beauty"

---

[70] Ibid; page 65
[71] Ibid; page 51

"As our knowledge of Nature and her laws has increased, so has our understanding of many passages in the Bible been improved. The Bible called the earth "the round world"; yet for ages it was the most damnable heresy for Christian men to say the world is round; and, finally, sailors circumnavigated the globe, proved the Bible to be right, and saved Christian men of science from the stake." [72]

Matthew Maury Monument – Wash. DC

Maury makes extensive references to God, "the Creator" throughout his monumental work giving God proper credit as the Creator of all we see and often quoted scripture for support of scientific thoughts. Another example: "Who, therefore, can calculate the benign influence of this wonderful current upon the climate of the South? In the pursuit of this subject, the mind is led from nature up to the Great Architect of nature; and what mind will the study of this subject not fill with profitable emotions? Unchanged and unchanging alone, of all created things, the ocean is the great emblem of its everlasting Creator. "He treadeth upon the waves of the sea," [Job 9:8] and is seen in the wonders of the deep. Yea, "He calleth forth its waters, and poureth them out upon the face of the earth." [Amos 9:6] [73]

---

[72] "The Physical Geography of the Sea"; M.F. Maury; Harper and Brothers Pub; 3rd edition; 1855; page 74
[73] Ibid page 50

Maury recognized the Creator behind the creation and commented; "There is no more worthy or suitable employment of the human mind than to trace the evidences of design and purpose in the Creator, which are visible in many parts of the creation." [74]

Maury learned good practices from his father who gathered his children together each day in the morning and night to read from the Bible. Maury's interest grew and he became so familiar with the Psalms of David that years afterward he could give a quotation and cite chapter and verse as though he had the Bible before him. [75]

---

[74] Ibid page 68

[75] "Matthew Fontaine Maury"; Charles Lewis; United States Naval Institute; published 1927; page 4

Chapter 4.3

Air Has Mass

Job 28:25
"*When He imparted **weight to the wind**, and meted out the waters by measure.*"
(NAS)

Weight (Hebrew: *mishqal*) Definition: heaviness, weight; Strong's #4948
Wind (Hebrew: *ruwach*) Definition: wind, breath, mind, spirit;   Strong's #7307

Shock wave causes condensation as this F-18 Hornet exceeds Mach 1

Weight of Air:

It isn't obvious to most folks but the air really has weight or more technically, mass. Density of air is a critical factor in aerodynamics and airplanes can't fly without some weight to the air. Denoted by the Greek symbol rho (ρ) it figures prominently in the aerodynamic lift and drag equations (lift = ½ * ρ * velocity^2 * lift coefficient * wing area). Air density drops off as you go higher into the atmosphere and that's why it is difficult to fly above 100,000 feet (most commercial aircraft fly around 35,000 feet or about 7 miles in the air). Density drops with temperature which makes it more difficult to land on very hot days like in Phoenix, Arizona where aircraft land 20 mph faster than normal because of this.

By the way, even though air has weight, it isn't a lot. Standard sea level air is about 0.076 lbs/ft^3.

Chapter 4.4

Springs of the Great Deep

Job 38:1-3, 16-17 (See also 2 Samuel 22:16 and Genesis 7:11)
"Then the LORD answered Job out of the storm. He said: [2] *"Who is this that darkens my counsel with words without knowledge?* [3] *Brace yourself like a man; I will question you, and you shall answer me......* [16] *Have you journeyed to the **springs of the sea** or walked in the **recesses of the deep**?* [17] *Have the gates of death been shown to you? Have you seen the gates of the shadow of death?"* (NAS)

Springs; (Hebrew; *nebek*) definition: springs; an unusual word used only once in scripture from an unused root meaning to "burst forth" – Strong's #5033

Sea; (Hebrew; *yam*) definition; sea or a specific sea (Mediterranean, Red Sea…); Strong's #3220

Deep (Hebrew; *thom*); definition: deep, depths, deep places, abyss, the deep, sea – Strong's #8415

Revelation to Job (circa 2,000 BC).

You know that phrase; "don't go there"? Well, if you ever get into the mood where you think you know better and want to tell God what He should be doing, Job was one of the first guys who "went there." As a result he would quickly now say don't. Job is probably the oldest book in the bible, estimated to have been written about 400 to 500 years before Moses, (Moses wrote the first five books of scripture around the time of the Exodus, which was about 1445 BC [76]) and after a period of time where Job continued to try to explain how much he knew about how things worked to several of his friends, God stepped in and put Job in his place. Recorded in several chapters in Job starting in 38, God makes some startling revelations. They are startling even to us today. One however, was left undiscovered for some 4,000 years. God spoke of springs of the sea (or deep) and the recesses of the deep. It wasn't

---

[76] "The Bible Expositional Commentary-OT-Genesis-Deut"; Warren Wiersbe; Victor – Cook Communications; copyright 2001; page 185

until the late 20th century that man has been able to explore the last liquid frontier. And guess what? In the great depths of the ocean, there are springs.

Smokers

"In 1977, scientists discovered hot springs at a depth of 2.5 km, on the Galapagos Rift (spreading ridge) off the coast of Ecuador." [77] This discovery had been anticipated since around 1970's because of oozing magma around the mid Atlantic ridge. These amazing hot water springs are around 400 degrees C (752 F) which well exceeds the boiling point of water, however the extreme pressure at these depths prevents the formation of gasses (or bubbles). Referred to as "smokers" they spew dark smoke like liquid which is mineral rich water. A great surprise was also the discovery of the amazing sea life that was apparently thriving around these vents. Included are giant tube worms, huge clams, and mussels.

Fountains of the Great Deep (Genesis 7:11):

We also know today that there are some very significant underground or subterranean chambers filled with water. This too would have been a shock to Job. Geologists Dr. Steve Austin points out that this is also anticipated in Psalm 33:6-9. Austin: "So, from the beginning of the creation, this passage is saying that the waters of the sea were heaped together. In characteristic Hebrew style this is rephrased in Psalm 33:7b as, "He lays up the deeps in

---

[77] http://pubs.usgs.gov/publications/text/exploring.html

storehouses." So, there is some vessel which is containing a portion of the deeps from the original creation." [78]

"Smoker"

Extra

Oh by the way, I don't think anyone has found the "gates of death" yet (or at least come back and tell us about it).

Gates (Hebrew *sha`ar*) definition; gate (of entrance); Strong's #8179)

Death (Hebrew maveth) definition: death, dying, Death (personified), realm of the dead; Strong's #4194

---

[78] See Institute for Creation Research; Impact #98 – "Springs of the Ocean" which can be found on: http://www.icr.org/article/180/

4 – Earth Sciences

Typically I reject most of the reports of those who claim to have been dead and returned to life because their reports of everything will be "OK" and we all make it to heaven are contrary to scripture. There is one however, that I find very fascinating. Don Piper is a strong "Born again" knowledgeable Christian and his account of "90 Minutes in Heaven" appears to be very consistent with scripture. He makes note of and comments on the "Gates of Heaven" [79] and it would seem reasonable to me to assume that if Heaven has a gate, then the Hades would as well. Just a thought.

Perplexing – isn't it!

---

[79] Piper describes the "Gate of Heaven"; "but was pearlescent – perhaps iridescent may be more descriptive. To me, it looked as if someone had spread pearl icing on a cake. The gate glowed and shimmered. I paused and stared at the glorious hues and shimmering shades. The luminescence dazzled me, and I would have been content to stay at that spot."; "Selection from - 90 Minutes in Heaven"; Don Peper; Revell Pub; copyright 2004, 2008; page 68-69

Chapter 4.5

The Barge of Noah

Genesis 6:13-16
*"Then God said to Noah, "The end of all flesh has come before Me; for the earth is filled with violence because of them; and behold, I am about to destroy them with the earth. "Make for yourself an **ark of gopher wood;** you shall make the ark with rooms, and shall cover it inside and out with pitch. "And this is how you shall make it: the length of the ark **three hundred cubits, its breadth fifty cubits, and its height thirty cubits**. "You shall make a **window** for the ark, and finish it to a cubit from the top; and set the door of the ark in the side of it; you shall make it with **lower, second, and third decks.**"* (NAS)

What's an Ark??

Ark: (Hebrew – *tebah*) definition: vessel – Strong's # 8392

Tebah is used in the Bible only in Genesis account referring to Noah's Ark a total of 26 times and twice in Exodus (2:3 & 2:5) referring to the basket that baby Moses was placed into and floated in the Nile. Further light is shed on the insights to *tebah* by the NIDOTTE: "Considering the size of Noah's Ark, the least ambiguous rendering is to call it a ship or large boat that retained a box-like appearance." [80] The word "Ark" is really a misnomer being that *tebah* is a different Hebrew word than the "Ark" of the covenant which is *aron* in Hebrew meaning chest or box (Strong's #727).

Perhaps the Forerunner of all Great and Magnificent Engineering Projects!

> Folks have a tendency to view the people of Noah's time as "primitive" and just above Neanderthals. Not even close! Noah was only 10 generations from the most perfect specimen of mankind that ever lived, Adam. If Noah lived in our day, he would probably be the most brilliant, intelligent and wise person walking the planet. He was close to physical and mental perfection; we live well over 100 generations later, having been constantly and slowly suffering from the degenerating effects of the curse.

Imagine for a moment, things have been rather difficult for the past several years. Seems like everything is going down hill so fast, you are afraid that in not to long a time there will be nothing left of value. You and your family have been very concerned and you are literally, not sure you will survive. It seems the company will close soon and that will probably bring the end to the entire area. There is a call, it is the General Manger. You meet with him in his office. He passes you a message and assignment that seems utterly preposterous. He tells you that you are now assigned to work directly for him and are to run one of the largest construction projects you have ever heard of. You ask him if this will save the company. The answer isn't what you expected. "This project will only save you and your family. No one else will want to join you." Shocking! Provided only with the basic dimensions and put on a schedule that seems impossible, you leave the office, clearly disturbed. Over time you come to understand the wisdom of the decision and program but that doesn't ease the burden of the job at hand. The project is immense and the logistical needs are staggering. Over the next several days, you work with your three foremen and a plan emerges. It will be tight, but it looks feasible. A few of the tasks seem unsolvable but gratefully, the General Manger has taken those off your plate and additionally, he has committed to make the necessary resources available and has put them at your disposal. This is what you have so far:

---

[80] "New International Dictionary of Old Testament Theology and Exegesis – Vol 4"; Willem Van Gemeren General Editor; Zondervan; copyright 1997; page 270

	Man Years	Comment
Initial Planning	**1**	What program manager or engineer would start without one
Ark Design	**78**	
Design Engineering and Drawings	10	This was my first engineering job
Structural Analysis	10	The Titanic was built without the aid of computers
Materials development and testing		The materials & process guys are the best
Wood selection	2	Difficult selection between ease of work and strength
Adhesives	4	I assume they were dealing with organics
Sealing techniques	2	It has to work
Structural tests (joints and design)	2	Unsung heroes
Water floating, balancing verification	2	Fabricate Scale models and test
Engineering Liaison during Fabrication	46	15% of Fabrication labor
Logging & Lumber	**174**	
Design improved cutting equipment	2	Modern mill can make 450 bdft/day/person; I used 77
Construct Mill	10	Design and build
Cut trees	30	You will clear over 250 acres of forest
Moved to "Mill"	20	Horse draw wagons
Mill – lumber	100	Need about 3 million board feet trimmed (using Douglas Fir)
Move to site	12	Move well over 4,000 tons of trimmed wood
Logistics	**37**	
Food Storage experiments	4	Storage methods needed to be developed (you will be on the ark over a year)
Feeding experiments (who eats what)	4	Needed to make sure the animals survived
Water feeding/quantity experiments	2	Probably would want to bring on board rather that collect rain
Gathering/growing food	15	Mostly done in the last year
Loading food stores and water	12	
Fabrication	**371**	
Fabrication Planning and Instructions	5	
Crew hiring, supervising	31	10% of Fabrication labor
Fab. tooling, cranes and wood transport equip.	25	
Fabrication of Adhesive	20	
Fabricate Ark	260	
Inspection	31	10% of Fabrication labor
Contingency	**66**	10% of total job (after all, this is the first time)
Total labor to design, build and outfit the Ark	**727**	Man years (done in 125 years) Need a crew of 6 people

Labor Estimate for Designing, Building and Outfitting the Ark

Dimensions of the Ark:

Length: 300 cubits   Breath: 50 cubits   Height: 30 cubits
Most folks make a conservative estimate using a cubit = 18 inches
Length: 450 feet   Breath: 75 feet   Height: 45 feet
Hebrew historian Josephus around the time of Christ stated the ancient cubit was equal to 21 inches. [81]
Length: 525 feet   Breath: 88 feet   Height: 53 feet
Jewish scholar Ben-Uri suggests a "long cubit" = 50 cm = 19.7 inches [82]

Significance of the Numbers: [83]

- 3 – Number of **divine perfection**; God's attributes (omniscient, omnipresent, omnipotent), time (past, present and future), matter (animal, vegetable and mineral), resurrection (3rd day land came up from water came up – Gen 1:10; 3rd day Jesus rose; 3rd day Joshua rose from the sea monster – Matt 12:39) (page 107)
- 7 – Number of **spiritual perfection**: 7 days of creation, 7 lamps on the golden lampstand in the Temple, (page 107)
- 10 – Perfection of **divine order**: or ordinal perfection; 10 commandments, Lord's Prayer has 10 clauses, tithe (page 243)
- 50 – **Jubilee** or Deliverance: it is the issue of 7^2 ($7^2+1=50$) (page 268)
- 30 – Higher degree of **perfection of Divine Order** = 3 x 10; Christ starts ministry at 30 years of age (Luke 3:23), Joseph also 30 when elevated (Gen 41:46), David was 30 when he took over (2 Sam 5:4)
- 300 – **Magnitude higher of Divine Order** = 3 x 10^2

300 x 50 x 30; Dimensions are all multiples of the divine ordinal number of 10; Length being an emphatic divinely ordered number with 3, the divine perfection; Breath implies deliverance; and Height is a divine ordinal with divine perfection.

---

[81] "Noah's Ark – Fact or Fable?"; Violet M Cummings; Creation Science Research Center; copyright 1972; page 72
[82] "Noah's Ark: A Feasibility Study"; John Woodmorappe; Institute for creation Research; copyright 1996; page 10
[83] "Number in Scripture"; E. W. Bullinger; Kregel Pub.; copyright 1967; first published in 1895

Hagopinan Configuration of the Ark (Barge)

Noah

Genesis 6:8 *"But Noah found **grace** in the eyes of the LORD."* (KJV)
First mention of the word "grace"

Grace: (Hebrew – chen (from #2603 graciousness); definition: favor, grace, pleasant or prescious – Strong's #2580
Noah: (Hebrew – *Noach*); definition: rest or comfort – Strong's 5146

Jesus: *"Come to Me, all who are weary and heavy-laden, and I will give you **rest** [Noah]."* (NAS) Matt 11:28

Noah the Prophet:
Noah lived in ancient times and was singled out by God to warn the world of a coming judgment. His life was characterized by his;

Righteousness, Faith, Obedience & Courage

Born in a time of oppressive wickedness, Noah distinguished himself with a Godly lifestyle to become one of the three most righteous men to ever live (Ezek 14:14,20). Yet his monumental righteousness was insufficient to save him from the judgment that came upon the entire world. It was his faith in the God of Heaven that preserved him (Heb 11:7). Noah was a fourth generation preacher who faithfully preached of God's coming judgment. With unimaginable courage and unwavering faith, he declared to a lost world their need for salvation. Noah faithfully proclaimed the Word of the Lord for 125 years even though no one responded to his call. Of how many men can it be said, "He did all that God had commanded him" (Gen 6:22). Noah's life of great faith lead him to become the "Heir of Righteousness" showing us the path, by faith, where we, who live in Christ will co-reign with Him, who is the "Heir of All Things" (Heb 1:2; 2Tim 2:12).

Mountains of Ararat   **Rare Photo of Noah**

James says "I will show you my faith by what I do" (Jam 2:18).
Noah's faith was in his driveway,
and it was 450' long, 75' wide and 45' high!!

Engineering of the Barge (Ark):

It is difficult to grasp and visualize the size and immensity of the Ark. It is just plain really big. John Woodmorappe has done an excellent job in conducting a feasibility study of all the logistical aspects of the voyage. He carefully calculates the animals, their size, how much space they need, what water they needed and including a detailed study of the care and feeding of all theses animals. [84] Check it out if you would like more details in this area. The table below is a summary of his calculations for the entire vessel and its cargo. We can get a pretty good idea of the total "draft" or weight by the water displaced from Genesis 7:20 which tells us that the water covered the high mountains by 15 cubits (22 feet). This suggests that the Ark had a draft of something just under this, probably 15' to up to perhaps 20'. 15 feet yields a total weight of close to 17,000 lbs while a 20' draft would yield about 21,000 tons. This is a pretty big barge.

Weight (tons)	Item
4,000	Empty weight of the ark
111	Animals (Ended at 411 tons)
2,500	Food
4,070	Water
6,000	Spares
16,681	**Total weight at start of voyage**
16,200	Draft of 10 cubits (15') on Ark

Stability of the craft:

George W. Dickie, a great marine architect and designer of the Spanish American War era, designed the battleship "Oregon" (1893) using the dimensions of Noah's Ark. Dickie stated he had got the idea for the proportions for the battleship 'Oregon' from the bible. "He figured that God gave Noah these directions knowing that it would have to withstand the roughest sea that would ever strike this world and the any typhoon that we would have today would be child's play in comparison. So, Mr. Dickie was confident that although these dimensions would make a very clumsy looking boat, according to modern ideas, he knew that this would be able to perform its work and be invincible." [85] In his research on this subject, he figured a cubit to be 22 inches. The mighty 'Oregon' was an 86% model of the Ark and performed well during an incredible storm on a cruise to Manila and during a typhoon later.

---

[84] "Noah's Ark – A Feasibility Study"; John Woodmorappe: Institute for Creation Research; Copyright 1996

[85] "Noah's Ark – Fact or Fable"; Violet M Cummings; Creation Science Research Center; copyright 1972; page 80

U. S. S. Oregon.

Marine Architect George Dickie designed the Battle Ship "Oregon" using the dimensions of Noah's Ark expressing confidence that even though "clumsy" looking, it would be very stable (it is an 86% scale)

Configuration:

No one knows for sure what the configuration of the Ark was/is. I believe the most likely is the Hagopinan configuration. Amazing first and second hand accounts over the past several hundred years are carefully chronicled in Cummings book "Noah's Ark – Fact or Fable" [86] and I think it makes a compelling case for this or something similar.

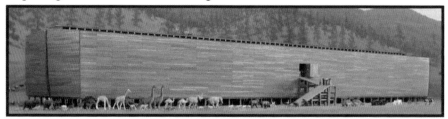

Hagopinan Configuration

Several folks have suggested configurations that look more like modern ships. These tend to have pointed bows and sterns to reduce drag as they are powered through the waters. Presumably the Ark had no motor and therefore had no

---

[86] ""Noah's Ark – Fact or Fable"; Violet M Cummings; Creation Science Research Center; copyright 1972

need of a "slippery" design. Never-the-less, proponents of this configuration are spurned on by some who claim that a formation near the base of Mt. Ararat is actually the fossilized remains of the Ark itself. Opponents abound in favor of legends of the Ark on the Mountain of Ararat itself, buried in a glacier. Perhaps time will tell.

An extremely novel and very provocative configuration has been suggested that takes advantage of a little aerodynamics. [87] During heavy seas, the amount of heaving and rolling can significantly be reduced (making the ride much smoother) by steering the ship directly into the waves. When you take waves on the side, the shorter dimension, there can be considerably rolling action making the passengers very uncomfortable (seasick). Waves are almost always coming from the direction of the wind (indeed – it is the wind that generates them) so steering into the waves is synonymous with steering into the wind. A clever way to accomplish that is to have a "vertical tail" or more accurately, a sail at the end of the boat. It would act like a turning vane and keep the craft pointed into the wind. I believe this would have made the ride much more tolerable during the early part of the flood when the storms raged and our current atmosphere was being established.

---

[87] Configuration suggested by folks at WorldWideFlood.com:
http://www.worldwideflood.com/default.htm

4 – Earth Sciences

"Gopher" Wood ???:

Genesis 6:14
"Make for yourself an ark of __gopher wood__; you shall make the ark with rooms, and shall cover it inside and out with pitch."

Gopher: (Hebrew – gopher) Definition – Unknown – Strong's # 1613; the word is used only once in the bible and this is it.

Understanding the word *"gopher"* is a perplexing problem for translators and many just leave the Hebrew word untranslated. Several have suggested Cypress, others Teak, but these are only guesses based on what is a good ship building wood.

A few have suggested that this is a scribal error! [I am always very slow to accept this as an explanation] Their thought is that the first letter in *gopher* (Gimmel) is very similar to the first letter in *kopher* (Kaph) (*kopher* meaning pitch) and suggesting that it is an emphasis of the "pitch" which occurs later in the sentence. Remember, Hebrew reads from right to left.

גֹּפֶר gopher {go'-fer}   כֹּפֶר kopher {ko'-fer} pitch

Others have suggested that gopher is a process, not a type of wood. This is extremely provocative. One of the most intriguing is "laminating." Technically, this makes a lot of sense. Thinner layers could be use and bonded or laminated one on top of the other, like plywood only built in place. As an old composite structures person (graphite/epoxy and glass/epoxy) I love the idea of laminated structures.

	Strength (psi)					(psi)
	Tension //	Horizontal shear	Comp. ⊥	Comp. //	Modulus	Extreem fiber bending
Douglas Fir	1,100	85	455	1,300	1.70E+06	1,900
Ply - Douglas Fir	2,000	240	1,375	1,460	1.60E+06	1,875

Construction difficulty is greatly reduced when building a "Monocoque" type structure rather than a "truss" or "space frame" which are alternate concepts. Monocoque structures are typically stronger, lighter and stiffer that other design techniques. Laminated or "plywood" is nearly twice as strong as the same wood which is not laminated. [88]

---

[88] Marks' Standard Handbook for Mechanical Engineers; Theodore Baumeister – Editor-in-chief; McGraw-Hill Book Company; first edition 1916; 8th edition; copyright 1978; see pages 6-128 and 6-135

However, as much as I am enthused by laminating, what is the justification from the text? Several folks have noted that the word gopher has come forward today and lives in its same, basic original form. "In the Concise Oxford Dictionary 1954 edition under the word 'gofer, gaufre, goffer, gopher, and gauffer see also wafer' it speaks of a number of similar things ranging from wafers as in biscuit making (layers of biscuit) or in a honeycomb pattern, to layers of lace in dressmaking, and hence goffering irons to iron the layers of lace." [89]

God calls the Ark out for "Sea Trials"

---

[89] See: http://www.giveshare.org/BibleStudy/241.gopherwood-ark.html and also http://www.worldwideflood.com/ark/wood/gopher_wood.htm

Possible causes of the flood:

Whatever was the cause that God used to initiate the events that caused the worldwide flood, it must have been something significant. The strong language of 2 Peter 3 would suggest that more that just the earth was affected. In the next judgment by fire, the heavens and the earth are involved leaving the implication that the heavens were involved in the first judgment of the flood of the earth. Causal theories include (1) the catastrophic breakup of a planet between Mars and Jupiter where the asteroid belt is now located (2) earth being impacted by a large

asteroid (3) earth being impacted by an icy asteroid [90] (4) a near fly-by of a planet (Mars, Venus or interaction with Mercury & it's asteroids) (5) pre-stress in the earth's crust rose sufficiently to crack the crust. Pretty heavy stuff but it leads us to 2 Peter 3:5-6 *"....For when they maintain this, it escapes their notice that by the word* [logos] *of God the heavens existed long ago and the earth was formed out of water and by water, through which the world* [kosmos] *at that time was destroyed* [cataclysmed = inundated], *being flooded with water"* (NAS). The entire earth was formed (or re-formed) by the waters of the flood. A biblical fact that sadly, many Christian scientists still struggle with.

Background facts:

- The original land mass (pre Noah's flood) appears to be a single land mass, not divided into continents as it is today. (Gen 1:9) {divisions of the earth either occurred either at the time of the flood or shortly after the flood during the time of Peleg (Gen 10:25 - either 150 years [Masoretic Text] or about 500 years [LXX] later) }
- If the world as we know it was formed through the flood, the "high mountains" referred to in Genesis 7:19 (possibly only about 5,000 feet) that were covered (to a depth of 15 cubits {22 feet}) would not have included today's mountains like the Himalayas and Mt. Everest.

---

[90] Donald Patten, *The Biblical Flood and the Ice Epoc*; Seattle; Pacific Meridian Pub. 1966, ch's IV & VII

- If all the mountains and land was pushed into the sea filling the oceans' valleys and canyons, the average water depth would be about 1.7 miles deep of water covering all the earth [91] (example: the Pacific Ocean is about two miles deep on the average, while the continental US averages less than one mile above sea level) [92]
- 70% of the earth's surface is covered by water today

Where did the waters come from?

    An extremely heavy rain of even 1" per hour would only yield a flood of less than 100-foot depth over a 40 day period. As we saw in Section 4.1, the maximum possible amount of rain that the atmosphere can support is well less than 1%. The large bulk of the waters had to come from somewhere else.

Gen 7:11-12 "In the six hundredth year of Noah's life, in the second month, on the seventeenth day of the month, on the same day **all the fountains of the great deep burst open, and the floodgates of the sky were opened**. And the rain fell upon the earth for forty days and forty nights. (NAS)"

The "fountains of the deep" must have significantly played into equation. "Burst" is also a strong word suggesting very rapid and significant action. Several theories exist as to where the water came from and how it "burst open". This includes the concept that huge spaces of water existed either under the earth's surface or more possibly under the ocean floors surface and was shot forth when a rip or tear (large fissure) occurred in the earth above it. Analytical models of this arrangement have been built which account for an earth crust of about 10 miles thick over subterranean water chambers. Both dry land and mountains were on the surface along with the original sea. It is this 10-mile thick crust that would have ruptured releasing all the subterranean waters. [93]

---

[91] http://www.christiananswers.net/q-aig/aig-floodwater.html – *"Noah's Flood – Where did the water come from?"* copright 1966, 1999, 2000 Answers in Genesis - page 1 of 5

[92] http://www.ldolphin.org/flood.shtml – Lambert Dolphin, 1983 revised 1999, 2001, 2002

[93] *"In the beginning: Compelling Evidence for Creation and the Flood"*; Walt Brown; Center for Scientific Creation; copyright 1980, 2001 (7th edition); page 100

Canopy theories have been very popular for the past 20 years but have come under criticism in recent years. It was suggested that a dense canopy surrounded the earth creating a tropical type climate on the entire earth's surface prior to the flood. The thinking is that this canopy "collapsed" causing massive rains upon the earth. Recent analytical models of a canopy and this process have shown that a workable canopy could only hold the equivalent of about 6 feet of water.[94] While most scholars believe that there was a "canopy" above the earth that did create a tropical climate, it is only a partial contributor to the waters of the flood.

Another concept is that an icy asteroid (satellite of Mercury) entered the earth's atmosphere delivering massive amounts of water to the planet. Support for this idea derives from the fact that Saturn's rings consist of ice crystals and Venus atmosphere contains frozen ice crystals. [95]

Evidence is also mounting that there is still a huge amount of water stored deep in the earth in crystal lattices of minerals, which is possible because of the immense pressure.[96] This could have been part of the source of waters being released as well as part of the answer as to where the waters went.

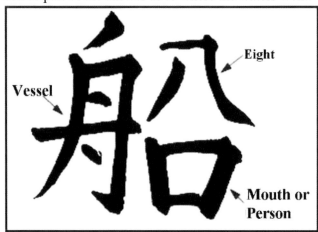

Chinese word for "Ship" is comprised of 3 roots, vessel, eight and person (or mouth) – Sounds like the "Ark"

[94] L. Vardiman, "The Sky Has Fallen", Proceddings fro mteh first ICC, 1986, 1:113-119 as quoted in "*Noah's Flood – Where did the water come from?*" page 4 of 7

[95] Donald Patten, *The Biblical Flood and the Ice Epoc*; Seattle; Pacific Meridian Pub. 1966, page 126

[96] L. Bergeron, "Deep waters," *New Scientist*, 1997, 155 (2097): 22-26

Where did the waters go?

Isa 54:9-10 *"For this is like the days of Noah to me; when **I swore that the waters of Noah should not flood the earth again**, so I have sworn that I will not be angry with you, nor will I rebuke you. For the mountains may be removed and the hills may shake, but My lovingkindness will not be removed from you, and My covenant of peace will not be shaken," says the LORD who has compassion on you."* (NAS) Isaiah leaves us with the impression that the earth's topography has changed sufficient so that however the flood was created, it can't be re-created. If the concepts of large underground (subterranean) water reservoirs broke free, is the cause of the flood, today they no longer exist in sufficient size or quantity to repeat the flood of Noah (although there is trapped water today below the surface).

Recognizing that the water of today's current oceans is sufficient to cover all the land of today, it is possible that all the water of Noah's flood is in today's oceans. If the crack or tear in the earth's crust released the subterranean waters, the crack would have torn continuously around the whole world at half the speed of sound. The crack becomes the Mid-Atlantic Ridge, continental drift begins and by hydroplate theory, current land masses emerge and the canyons of the deep oceans are formed drawing in the waters of the sea. Further, in this process, the mountains of today would have been lifted up at the time of the flood or shortly after it (the time of Peleg has been suggested). An alternative to the hydroplate theory is that of plate tectonics [97] although there are several issues associated with this approach. [98]

The language of Job 38:8-11 refers to the waves and the fact that God has put a

limit on them in terms of where they can go. Some scholars have suggested that the implication here is that these are the waters of Noah's flood and they have been limited since the flood. "If the waters are still here, why are the highest mountains not still covered with water, as they were in Noah's day? Psalm 104 suggests an answer. After the waters covered the

---

[97] http://www.answersingenesis.org/home/area/tools/flood-watersgo.asp – *"Where did the Flood waters go?*
[98] *"In the beginning: Compelling Evidence for Creation and the Flood"*; page 126

mountains (verse 6), God rebuked them and they fled (verse 7); the mountains rose, the valleys sank down (verse 8) and God set a boundary so that they will never again cover the earth (verse 9). They are the same waters!" [99]

Ps 104:5-9 *"He established the earth upon its foundations, so that it will not totter forever and ever. Thou didst cover it with the deep as with a garment; the waters were standing above the mountains. At Thy rebuke they fled; at the sound of Thy thunder they hurried away. The mountains rose; the valleys sank down to the place which Thou didst establish for them. Thou didst set a boundary that they may not pass over; that they may not return to cover the earth."* (NAS)

Summary of Noah's Waters and Personal Opinion

I think that God used some type of significant event such as a close fly-by of another planet or large asteroid strike to trigger and crack the earth's crust and initiate the flood of Noah's time. I personally think that most of the water required to cover the earth was already within the earth (subterranean waters) and it was just released because of a large earthquake or perhaps literally a break caused by a cosmic strike. I think this is reflected in the phrase of the waters "bursting forth". The planet becomes covered by the release of all this water. At this point, hydroplate theory comes in. The large landmasses under the waters are now very free to move about. The land masses shift an move opening up the huge rifts or canyons in the ocean floors and the waters begin to collect there. The land once again emerges. The land is still somewhat movable being saturated or "suspended" by water. Earth's plates continue to shift, sliding and bumping into each other pushing up all the new mountain ranges. This is evidenced in the fact that much of the earth's surface is

---

[99] ibid – page 5

comprised of layers of sedimentary rocks (even the Himalayas are sedimentary rocks containing extensive amounts of fossilized marine life) and many of the mountain ranges evidence the fact that the land has been folded upon it self. This concept would suggest that all the waters necessary for the flood were present within the earth's crust and left on the surface of the earth and after the flood. The waters have simply been collected in the extremely deep oceans today.

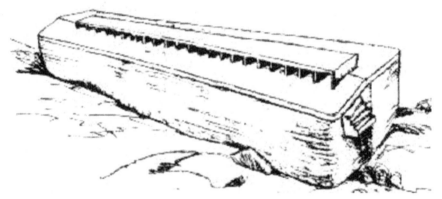

I believe that God chooses to limit Himself to the natural physical laws that he has established. I also believe that God set whatever events He used to kick-off the flood in motion at the beginning of creation. That is the amazing part of Gods plan. It is not changing and adjusting as we go along. He does not call audible plays (so to speak) at the line of scrimmage. He has planned out all these events and set them in motion at the instant of creation and their timing is impeccable, even perfect. For example, if the events were caused by an asteroid strike, God didn't bring it in from some distant galaxy at the last minute. It was set in a path at the beginning of creation so that at precisely the right time, it strikes the earth. My personal example is found in my annual mountain climbing adventure. Typically, at some point in my annual climb, I get in a difficult situation and pray and ask God to help me find a handhold or foothold to get me through the climb. I search for the path and have always found my route. Now, I don't believe that God pries open the rock while I am there. I believe that when God formed the rock mountain, He put in stresses and weak points and cracks in the rock. The tiny crack will fill up with water (from the snow and rains) every year. It freezes and in the freezing process, expands the crack ever so slightly. As summer comes followed by winter, the slightly larger crack is filled with water again, which freezes and expands once again. Over the hundreds of years, pretty soon there is a crack large enough for me to stick my hand into and use for climbing. I believe that when God formed the rock, He knew that I would come through and need help and He placed in the rock the necessary cracks to be formed over time to accommodate me when I would turn to Him for help. Pretty miraculous!! You bet. God has established the paths of our lives before the universe was formed. He prepared good works for us to do in advance. (Eph 2:10)

Doesn't it create an interesting thought that when we go surfing in the ocean, we are riding the waves of Noah's flood.

Where is the Ark today?

There is a lot of information out there; a lot of controversy and a lot contradictions. Bottom line for me, I think there is a reasonable possibility that the Ark actually survives to this day but God has not allowed it to be revealed yet. Perhaps it will be one day so it once again will be a sign to a generation about to be judged and condemned. Robert Cornuke has a recent book, which summarizes much of the searches for the ark in modern times and provides good insight revealing the possibility of a future ark discovery. [100]

I like what Forssberg says:

Forssberg's "Dissertation on the Ark" is the most fascinating and comprehensive compilation of facts and conjectures concerning the ark of the older books (1943). Forssberg talked about a tradition from the environs of Mount Ararat as follows: "If the hero can brave the icy crevasses and the devils that haunt them, and can scrape a little pitch from the timbers of the sacred vessel, he becomes invulnerable to the bullets and daggers of his enemies and the hearts of the fair sex are as wax before him." [101]

Man – who wouldn't want the hearts of the fair sex to melt before him? Who wants to go exploring?

---

[100] "Lost Mountain of Noah"; Robert Cornuke and David Halbrook; Broadman and Holman Pub; copyright 2001
[101] "Noah's Ark – Fact or Fiction"; Cummings; page 82

Chapter 4.6

Dragons and Dinosaurs

Job 40:15-24

*"Behold now, **Behemoth**, which I made as well as you; He eats grass like an ox. Behold now, his strength in his loins, and his power in the muscles of his belly. **He bends his tail like a cedar**; the sinews of his thighs are knit together. His bones are tubes of bronze; His limbs are like bars of iron. He is the first of the ways of God; let his maker bring near his sword. Surely the mountains bring him food, and all the beasts of the field play there. Under the lotus plants he lies down, in the covert of the reeds and the marsh. The lotus plants cover him with shade; the willows of the brook surround him. If a river rages, he is not alarmed; He is confident, though the Jordan rushes to his mouth. **Can anyone capture him when he is on watch, with barbs can anyone pierce his nose**?"* (NAS)

The Behemoth's description is more depictive of a dinosaur than any other animal that we know.

Behemoth

Behemoth: (Hebrew – behemoth); a kind of animal – Strong's #930 (used once in the bible)

It has been difficult to identify this magnificent beast. In a dialogue with Job, God selects two animals to make His point contrasting the greatness of God versus man. So, we expect to find that the Behemoth is among the most awesome of all God's creation. Scriptural translators really don't know what the "Behemoth" is and "this animal has been variously identified as an elephant, a hippopotamus, and a water buffalo, with the hippopotamus the more likely....based on the description." [102] However, in an objective look, can any of these animals really fit the description in Job? Does a hippopotamus sway his tail like a cedar? Perhaps a dinosaur would be a better fit to the description?

Leviathan

Job 41:1-10; see also Job 3:8; Psalm 74:14; 104:26; Isaiah 27:1

"Can you draw out Leviathan with a fishhook? Or press down his tongue with a cord? Can you put a rope in his nose? Or pierce his jaw with a hook? Will he make many supplications to you? Or will he speak to you soft words? Will he make a covenant with you? Will you take him for a servant forever? Will you play with him as with a bird? Or will you bind him for your maidens? Will the traders bargain over him? Will they divide him among the merchants? Can you fill his skin with harpoons, or his head with fishing spears? ___Lay your hand on him; remember the battle; you will not do it again! Behold, your expectation is false; will you be laid low even at the sight of him? No one is so fierce that he dares to arouse him; who then is he that can stand before me___?" (NAS)

Leviathan (Hebrew livyathan); "serpent"; a sea monster or dragon; Strong's #3882 (page 3839) – used 6 times

Have you ever seen a creature like this? This creature of old must have struck fear in the hearts of all mariners to catch a glimpse of this huge, monstrous

---

[102] Holman Illustrated Bible Dictionary"; Brand, draper and England Editors; Holeman pub; copyright 2003; page 183

animal navigating the oceans. Holman Bible Dictionary describes the Leviathan as; "Name of an ancient sea creature, meaning "coiled one," subdued by God…a sea creature as too formidable a foe for a person to consider arousing. [103]

Leviathan – possibly the "*Kronosaurus*" which is substantially larger and more powerful than that of the greatest carnivorous dinosaur, Tyrannosaurus" or the "*Pliosaur*" (55-66 feet in length and weighing 50 tons)

Dragons (Dragons in the KJV; Sea Monster or Serpent in the NAS and NIV)

Genesis 1:21; see also Job 7:12; Jer 51:34; Ezek 29:3; 32:2; Psalm 74:13; Psalm 148:7; Ex 7:12

"*And **God created the great sea monsters** [dragon], and every living creature that moves, with which the waters swarmed after their kind, and every winged bird after its kind; and God saw that it was good.*" (NAS)

Dragon (Hebrew *tannin*); Serpent, dragon or sea monster; Strong's #8577 used 14 times in the Old Testament (page 1491)

In 1611, the King James Version (KJV) translators translated the Hebrew word "*tannin*" into "**dragon**." It is used 14 times in the Old Testament. But what is a "dragon." In 1841 (over 200 years later) British anatomist coined the word "dinosaur" combining two Greek words *deinos* and *sauros* , which means "terrible lizard." [104] Therefore, we will not see the word "dinosaur" in the Bible, but is there any similarity between "dragon" and "dinosaur"?

---

[103] "Holeman Bible Dictionary"; page 1028

[104] "The Great Dinosaur Mystery – Solved"; Ken Ham; Master Books; copyright 1998; page 32

Mythical Dragon   Dinosaur

Interesting Dragon / Dinosaur Facts:

- Baryonyx; Discovery of a 12" long curved claw in Suxxex, England subsequently led to the recovery of a newly identified dinosaur about 30' in length and 10'-12' in height. On display in the Natural History Museum in London, it bears some remarkable similarities to the old English tales of dragons. [105]
- One of the oldest books of British History, "The Anglo-Saxon Chronicles" includes many encounters between people and dragons with descriptions that fit well-known dinosaurs. [106]

WALES

- Summary of some dragon legends: [107]
- Sumerian story (3000 BC) tells of Gilgamesh encountering a vicious dragon in the forest which he slays
- China has been renowned for its dragon stories (captured in stories, pottery, embroidery and carvings
- English story of St. George who slays a dragon in a cave

---

[105] "The Great Dinosaur Mystery – Solved"; page 35-37
[106] "The Early History of Man – Part 4. Living Dinosaurs from Anglo Sanon and other Early Records" as quoted in "The Great Dinosaur Mystery – Solved"; page 136
[107] "The Great Dinosaur Mystery - Solved"; page 38

- 10th century Irishman wrote of his encounter of what appears to have been a *stegosaurus*.
- "Historia Animalium"; a 1500's European scientific book lists several live animals which to us are dinosaurs.

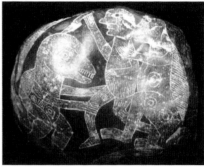

Above are pictures of some controversial Peruvian pottery that has been dated to be about 700 years old, well before the discovery of any dinosaur bones. Depicted are soldiers riding on or fighting what appear to be as dinosaurs.

Scientists at the University of Montana found T-rex bones that were not totally fossilized! There is no way that bones that are millions of years old can not be totally fossilized. Their report states; "the lab filled with murmurs of amazement, for I had focused on something inside the vessels that none of us had ever noticed before: tiny round objects, translucent red with a dark center…red blood cells? The shape and location suggested them, but blood cells are mostly water and couldn't possibly had stayed preserved in the 65-million-year-old tyrannosaur…the bone sample from a beautiful, nearly complete specimen of *Tyrannosaurus rex* unearthed in 1990…but more work needs to be done before we are confident enough to come right out and say, 'Yes, this T. *rex* has blood compounds left in its tissues.'" [108]

---

[108] "The Real Jurassic Park"; Schweitzer and Staedter; page 55-57 as quoted in "The Great Dinosaur Mystery – Solved" ; page 18-19

Malachi 1:3
"And I hated Esau, and laid his mountains and his heritage waste for the dragons of the wilderness." (KJV)
Wow, the dragons (Strong #8568 – *tannah* – translated as Jackal in the NAS and NIV) destroy the mountain wilderness of Esau.

Isaiah 30:6
*"The burden of the beasts of the south: into the land of trouble and anguish, from whence [come] the young and old lion, the viper, **the flying serpent**, hey will carry their riches upon the shoulders of young asses, and their treasures upon the bunches of camels, to a people that shall not profit [them]."*
There are different species of Pteranodon and they can have up to a 53-foot wing span weighting up to 40 lbs. As it turns out, the Pteranodon would have had a very difficult time flying in our atmosphere because of its wingspan to weight ratio. If there was a canopy around the earth as indicated in Genesis, the atmosphere could have been over twice as dense enabling smooth flight for the Pteranodon. [109]

Even though he is speaking figuratively, Isaiah is referencing real animals.

---

[109] "The Waters Above"; Joseph Dillow; Moody Press; copyright 1981; page 147-150

Conclusion:

Are there really dinosaurs in the Bible? Good question and certainly very controversial. Clearly, there are ancient words used in the Bible that we are unable to link with modern animals, which doesn't say necessarily that there are necessarily dinosaurs. Certainly there were animals that are now extinct. However, the descriptions in Job are too close to dinosaurs and too far from anything we know to make it likely that they are modern animals. In addition, the fact that God highlights the Behemoth and the Leviathan would indicate to me that these must be some of the more awesome creatures. This does not jive with a hippo to me. I am inclined to think that these are descriptions of what we refer to today as dinosaurs. "The New International Dictionary of Old Testament Theology and Exegesis" states concerning the word tannin [dragon]; "From Ezek 29:3 and 32:2 many deduce that the crocodile or the hippopotamus is intended. Yet a greater and mightier sea creature is more likely." [110]

---

[110] "New International Dictionary of Old Testament Theology and Exegesis – Vol 4"; Willem Van Gemeren General Editor; Zondervan; copyright 1997; page 314

4 – Earth Sciences

Chapter 4.7

The Capacity of God

Matthew 10:29 (see also Luke 12:6)
"Are not two sparrows sold for a cent? And yet not one of them will fall to the ground apart from your Father." (NAS)

Cent (Greek *assarion*) definition: an assarium or assarius, the name of a coin equal to the tenth part of a drachma; or the smallest copper coin of the time; Strong's #787

Sparrow (Greek strouthion) definition: a little bird, esp. of the sparrow sort, a sparrow; Strong's #4765

Details

Don't let the familiarity of this verse cause you to miss the shocking revelation. God is so in tune, so involved, so active with His creation that the life of a tiny little sparrow does not go unnoticed. There is absolutely nothing in this entire universe that is not subject to the sovereignty of God, not even a tiny sparrow which will fit in the palm of your hand.

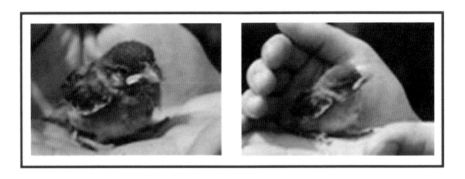

Jesus on birds: Luke 12:23-25

*"Life is more than food, and the body more than clothes. ²⁴Consider the ravens: They do not sow or reap, they have no storeroom or barn; **yet God feeds them**. And how much more valuable you are than birds! ²⁵Who of you by worrying can add a single hour to his life?"*

It is God Himself who makes sure that the animals are fed.

Chapter 5.1

Did Anyone Really Ever Believe the Earth was Flat?

Isaiah 40:22 – Also Prov 8:27; Amos 9:6; Job 26:7-10
*"It is He [God] who sits above **the circle of the earth**, and its inhabitants are like grasshoppers, Who stretches our the heavens like a curtain and spreads them out like a tent to dwell in."* (NAS)

Jesus, our Lord, is actively holding the universe (all things) together!

> **"Our misconceptions and preconceptions of history and scripture cloud our ability to understand what God is telling us in this area of cosmology"**

Circle (Hebrew - *khug*); definition – sphere

If the earth is flat, why doesn't all the water run off the edges? I never could figure that out. Why did people of the old days think the earth was flat? Well, as it turns out, most of the people didn't think that it was. From the 3rd century on, most people thought it was round. Jeffrey Russell's book "Inventing of the Flat Earth" [111] directly comes at this point and demonstrates rather conclusively that for Columbus, the issue was not "is the earth flat." It was, "is the distance too long to make the voyage"? However, the thought that the church opposed Columbus on biblical grounds of a "flat earth" is frequently used in criticism of the Scriptures. Russell clearly points out that the "flat earth error" continues to persist and most folks don't realize that the church really didn't oppose scientific development. And, while we are at it, what is that whole "earth is the center of the universe" thing. Is that what the bible teaches? It would seem pretty hard to maintain a position that the earth is the center of the solar system these days, even though there are some to still try. Let's take these two questions one at a time.

---

[111] "Inventing of the Flat Earth: Columbus and Modern Historians"; Jeffrey Russell; Praeger Pub; copyright 1991

Scriptures on a "flat" or "round" earth:

We don't fine anywhere in scripture a description of a "flat" earth anywhere in scripture. The only really direct reference to the subject is Isaiah. He refers to the subject and uses the Hebrew word *khug* in this passage which literally means "Sphere". This is another great area where scripture has given us scientific information unavailable at the time from other sources.

Replicas of Columbus' Ships

What is the story on Christopher Columbus? Although different than what we are typically taught in elementary school about the discoverer of the "New World" (Americas) in which we live today, Christopher Columbus had a profound faith in God, Christ and the scriptures. Columbus from an early age, felt predestined, chosen for a special mission by God. His name, Christ-Topher ("Christ-bearer"), he felt was evidence of his destiny. Passages of scripture provided him with a more compelling reason for his courageous voyage than any view of astronomy. His book entitled "Libro de las Profecias" ["Book of Prophecies"], written near the end of his life, quotes several biblical passages on the "Isles" of the sea which had driven him all his life. Columbus

110

clearly states that his discovery of the New World was "the fulfillment of what Isaiah prophesied." Columbus references Isaiah 24:15; "Isles beyond the sea," [NAS translates it "coastlands of the sea" – and footnotes "Islands"] and Isaiah 60:9.6. [112] Also included in Columbus' references were: Proverbs 8:27, which speaks of the earth's surface as being curved; Isaiah 40:22, the spherical earth; and the ocean currents in Isaiah 43:16. Just a few days after his discovery of the "New World" Columbus wrote the following in his journal: "Praise be to the eternal God our Lord, who gives to all those who walk in His ways victory over all things which seem impossible." [113] Surprising, Columbus, as the "Christ-bearer" was significantly motivated to bring the good news of the gospel to the natives for the purpose of their salvation. This, to some degree was initially accomplished, however, the colony and Columbus its leader quickly succumbed to the evil allure of wealth and their quest for gold took priority. [114]

Four Corners of the Earth:

What about the "Four Corners of the Earth"? Does that not imply that the earth is flat? Let's take a look.

Isaiah 11:12; See also Rev 7:1 & Rev 20:8
"And He will lift up a standard for the nations and assemble the banished ones of Israel, and will gather the dispersed of Judah from the **four corners of the earth**." [NAS]

Corners; (Hebrew – *kanaph*); definition- wing or wing extremity (of the 107 times the word in used in scripture, it is translated "wing" or related 77 times.) [115]

It is interesting that the Psalmist selected a word that is not descriptive of the corners of a paper, but rather the "wing" or sections an object such as the

---

[112] Article: "Columbus and His Creator" by Paul Humber – ICR – is located at http://www.icr.org/index.php?module=articles&action=view&ID=347 and gives some good background.

[113] "A Cloud of Witnesses"; Steven Northrop; First published Mason Long Publishing 1894; Mantle Ministries Pub (Reprint); page 95

[114] This well researched book gives an inspiring section on Columbus, his background and journey to the "New World"; "The Light and the Glory"; Peter Marshall & David Manuel; Revell – Baker Book House; copyright 1977; Chapters 1 & 2

[115] Strongs #1137; Zondervan NASB Exhaustive Concordance; Zondervan; Zondervan; copyright 1991 & 1998; page 1518

"wings" of a building, their extremities. Other Hebrew words could have been used; (1) "*miqtsoa*" (Strong's # 4740 – page 1428) used in describing the corners of the tabernacle meaning "corner" or "buttress" (2) "*peah*" (Strong's #6285 – page 1453) used in describing the corners of a field meaning "corner" or "side" (3) *pinnah* (Strong's #6438 – page 1455) used to describe towers on the corners of the city meaning "corner towers." Technically, the Psalmist is telling us that God will gather the Israelites from the extremities of the earth [typically meaning in relation to Jerusalem from where they were dispersed] and the verse doesn't imply a "flat earth."

Revelation 7:1
"After this I saw four angels standing at the four corners of the earth, holding back the four winds of the earth, so that no wind would blow on the earth or on the sea or on any tree."

Corners; (Greek – gonia); definition- an angle or a corner

This is a very challenging an insightful verse and there is potentially more than we think being communicated to us. It is not clear to me why "4 corners" are used here which would seem to imply something flat with 4 edges. Beyond the obvious use as perhaps just an expression; it is interesting that the verse is in context with "angels" which imply right away the spiritual dimension. We do know from other scriptures that the universe can be "rolled up", "torn" and "folded" which imply that in the hyperspace of the universe, there must be one dimension that is relatively "thin." If this is the case, we can conjecture that perhaps in the bigger picture of hyperspace, the angles are truly located in the "corners" of the earth.

Another interesting feature of this passage is that we can see the angels or spiritual beings being in control of the winds. If God's angels, then clearly at God's bidding. If evil creatures are the source, they act only with the permission of God. It is surprising to see the encounter that Jesus had one day on a boat (Matt 8:24). He was on the Sea of Galilee when unusually strong winds began to blow placing them all in danger of their very lives. Don't pass this over too quickly. Several of the disciples were fisherman and had spent most of their lives on this body of water. Whatever was happening to them clearly was beyond the more natural and they were terrified, in fear for their lives. Finding Jesus asleep in the back of the boat, the disciples become even more disturbed for His apparent lack of concern and they wake Him up. Jesus chastises the disciples for their lack of faith in crisis (especially after just having witnessing the miracle of feeding of the 4,000 people) and then Jesus "commands" the storm to be still. One does not give orders to an in adamant object. There is a spiritual power behind the weather and Christ has authority over it. In this example, He demanded immediate obedience and the spirits complied.

Scriptures on the Earth's Orbit:

Psalm 19:1-6;

" *[1] The heavens are telling of the glory of God; And their expanse is declaring the work of His hands. [2] Day to day pours forth speech, And night to night reveals knowledge. [3] There is no speech, nor are there words; Their voice is not heard. [4] Their line has gone out through all the earth and their utterances to the end of the world. In them He has placed a tent for the sun, [5] Which is as a bridegroom coming out of his chamber; [6] It rejoices as a strong man to run his course.* **Its [sun's]** *rising is from one end of the heavens and* **its circuit** *to the other end of them."* [NAS]

> Circuit; (Hebrew - *tequphah*); definition – "a coming round circuit" [116]

This is also a very challenging passage that, at first glance, seems to imply that the sun is revolving around the earth. The context of the passage is clearly cosmological, speaking of the universe that we see. Taking a close look, we see that the sun, like an athlete running a course, makes its circuit from one end of heaven to the other. The verse isn't telling us that the sun goes around the earth, it is describing a path for the sun "in the heavens." A circuit isn't necessarily circular; it just finishes in the same place it started. Like a race track, there are ovals, ellipticals and figure eight circuit tracks. We are not sure of the path of our solar system, but modern cosmologists suggest that we (our galaxy – with our solar system) are moving through the universe on some sort of path, and here, God tells us that it is a circuit. Amazing, how did the Psalmists of over 2,500 years ago know to describe an "orbit" for the sun.

Well, wait a minute. What about all those Middle Ages religious folks who seemed to think that the sun revolved around the earth? Where did they get that idea? It is true that folks like Copernicus and Galileo had a difficult time proposing their ideas that the sun was the center of the solar system and the

---

[116] Strong's #8622; "Zondervan NASB Exhaustive Concordance"; Zondervan; copyright 1991 & 1998; page 1491

earth revolved around it. It is important to note that this opinion was the predominate view in the science/religious community for the previous 2,000 years but it was not derived from the Scriptures. It was the teaching of the false philosophies of Aristotle and Ptolemy that were embraced by society and what these brave men faced. We should also clarify that is wasn't just persecution by the church that prevented these radical new ideas from going forward. There were intrigues and political agendas that were being worked, people who stood to lose influence that became roadblocks to embracing this understanding. [117] Martin Luther was one of those who gave opposition to the work of Copernicus in 1539. Although much is made of Luther's attacks on Copernicus, Luther's criticism was pretty straight forward. [118] Luther viewed the theory as reasonably unsupported and commented that Joshua commanded the sun to stand still during the battle of Beth Horon (Josh 10:12) and logically concluded that the scriptures taught that the sun was moving, not the earth. However, Luther is perhaps premature on this. Psalm 19 does not support the position that the sun is moving around the earth and the unbelievable miracle that God performed in Joshua's day is a poor one to be solely used to draw a far reaching conclusion. Joshua's account is extremely challenging for many reasons and we have great difficulty describing what took place. And that is really independent of what celestial body is moving around what. For more on the Joshua account, see section 5.6 – 360 day year. As history unfolded, we find that Johannes Kepler (a great scientists in his own right and a strong believer in God, the divine nature of scripture and their consistency with true science) clarified the Joshua's passage interpretation so that it was not contradictory with and earth revolving around the sun (however – it doesn't explain how the miracle happened – which remain only conjectures even today). However, the heliocentric planetary system (planets revolving around the sun) did not receive general scientific acceptance until Isaac Newton presented his gravitation laws and laws of mechanics which resolved many of the questions hindering this. [119]

---

[117] There is some great background on this issue in "The Galileo Connection"; Charles Hummel; InterVarsity Press; copyright 1986

[118] A good summary background on this subject is in an article by Donald Kobe; "Copernicus and Martin Luther: an encounter between science and religion," in American Journal of Physics – 66 (March 1998): 190-196. An excerpt can be found at http://www.leaderu.com/science/kobe.html#copernicus

[119] Ibid

5 – Astronomy and Cosmology

Chapter 5.2

Age of the Universe
7 Days versus 15 Billion Years

Exodus 20: 9-11
"Six days you shall labor and do all your work, but the seventh day is a sabbath of the LORD your God; in it you shall not do any work, you or your son or your daughter, your male or your female servant or your cattle or your sojourner who stays with you. **_For in six days the LORD made the heavens and the earth, the sea and all that is in them, and rested on the seventh day_**; *therefore the LORD blessed the sabbath day and made it holy."* (NAS)

Day: (Hebrew – *yowm*); definition: a day, literal or figurative – Strong's #3117

Earth's Age Controversy – Introduction:

Biblical prophecy concerning the beliefs of the "End Times" is being fulfilled and lived out in all public educational institutions today. In spite of overwhelming data evidencing a creator, public institutions continue to proclaim a known lie stating the life and the universe is a result of random chance. Christendom has divided itself on the beliefs of the age of the universe, and for this reason, presents to the world it is trying to help a confusing picture making it difficult to draw scientists or engineers into the truth. What is overlooked by most everyone involved in the controversy is the fact that emerging data from physics is once again clearly indicating that there is substantially more to this universe than we can detect with our five physical senses and it provides a potential solutions to the age of the universe which supports the Bible. My encouragement is to ask Christian scientists and engineers to take and objective look and consider the consequences of recent developments in the field of quantum physics. Congratulations are in order for all Christian scientists who have faithfully led the fight for the past 100 years against evolution. That battle is turning and being won on some limited fronts. Most secular scientists understand that even though the socially motivated leaders of the educational system refuse to change, it is becoming more difficult to defend traditional evolutionary model and many of the new ones. The faith of Christians to remain faithful to the truth revealed by scriptures of the God of Creation has proved to be well founded. It is my opinion that over the next several decades quantum physics will not only further illuminate the origin of the universe but also will provide supporting evidence of the Creator Beyond Time and Space as revealed through the Bible.

Impact of Evolutionary Thought:

The reformation created motive and industrial revolution created the opportunity for the spread of the bible from the 1600's through the 1800's. A large number of people were able to obtain regular access to scripture and it was well recognized as the "Words of God."

Fulfillment of prophecy, advanced scientific insight (hygiene, treatment of diseases, physical science information and other factors) created a strong case for Biblical origin outside our time/space continuum. This action led to extensive world missionary work in the late 1700's and 1800's as typified by such self sacrificing missionaries as Albert and Susan Sturges who gave much of their entire lives to live in unbelievable difficult conditions with the only objective of bringing Micronesian islanders to a saving relationship Jesus Christ.[120] The advancing Christian faith was countered in the later 1800's from initially within the church (which should not surprise us as we are repeatedly warned in scripture that false teachings will come from within the church (Jude, 2 Peter and Ephesians). Charles Darwin published his thoughts in a book entitled "The Origin of Species" which suggests life evolved from lower life forms to higher ones. In spite of his personal beliefs, the book, in effect, launched a major movement against the existence of God stating the universe was a result of random acts. Julian Huxley, an early and strong supporter of Darwin stated the emerging thoughts of the time: "It will soon be as impossible for an intelligent, educated man or woman to believe in a god as it is now to believe that the earth is flat." [121] The rise of the Totalitarian leaders Hitler,

---

[120] Their story is presented in "Missionary Adventures in the South Pacific"; David and Leona Crawford; Tuttle Pub; copyright 1967

[121] from "Religion without Revelation: J. Huxley; page 62; as quoted in "Baker - Encyclopedia of Christian Apologetics"; Norman Geisler: Baker; copyright 1999; 5th printing Dec 2000; page 345.

Lenin and Stain in the late 1800's and early 1900's gave credit to and praised Darwin for liberating them from encumbering theology. Karl Marx wished to dedicate his book to Darwin. [122] Evolutionary thought caused many to begin to question and dis-believe the bible and has prevented many from embracing biblical truths. If the first chapters of the bible which describe how God created the universe can not be trusted, why should any of it be trusted. Indeed, this seems a reasonable course of action except for a few factors. **One**: the bible does have substantial data demonstrating that it is from God (fulfilled prophecy and other scientific data) independent of the creation account. **Two**: Even though many attempt to present it a fact, evolution has always been a theory, and even though confidently stated by Darwin that the fossil record would contain extensive intermediary species this has failed to materialize. [123] Geological thought of the late 1800's began to describe the age of the earth in term of millions of years. Darwinists

Stygimoloch **skull**

embraced their thoughts as they began to recognize that a lot of time was necessary if evolution was to have taken place. Through the 1900's sociologists working their own agenda began to actively make evolution the only credible thought and they have successfully imbedded this false teaching into virtually all aspects of public education. In spite of the fact that virtually all scientific data discovered in the last 100 years overwhelmingly supports a creator rather that chance evolution. Included in these discoveries is: (1) no evolutionary supporting data in the massive fossil record unearthed in the last 100 years; (2) discovery that the "simple single cell" is anything but simple containing very sophisticated systems such as information storage, reproduction, movement mechanism, food capture and processing capability and (3) DNA research of the past 50 years showing among many things that all life has the same code of life (DNA) only it is programmed differently for each

---

[122] Lambert Dolphin: http://www.ldolphin.org/gould.html; page 3 of 4

[123] David Raup, curator of the Field Museum of Natural History in Chicago stated, "We are now about 120 years after Darwin and the knowledge of the fossil record has been greatly expanded. We now have a quarter of a million fossil species, but the situation hasn't changed much…We have even fewer examples of evolutionary transition than we had in Darwin's time." as quoted in "The Face that Demonstrates the Farce of Evolution"; Hank Hannegraaff; Word Pub; copyright 1998; page 34

species. The implication of this being that the code for all life forms exists in very simple cells organisms and would have had to be there from the very beginning making the first "evolutionary step" virtually a complete one for all life forms. Evolution has truly become a "Theory in Crisis." The wide spread rejection of a Creator, [124] incidentally, is prophesied in the bible as one of the indicators of the "last days." 2 Peter 3:3-6 states that people of the last days will view the universe as a stable and constant rejecting the concept that it was created by God.

Summarizing these thoughts, we find that availability of scripture and belief in the bible as the Word of God for several hundred years led to major expansion of Christianity. However, with the advent of evolutionary thought in the late 1800's, many oppressive cultures emerged embracing Darwinism as the justification for their approach of dominance by the advanced and powerful. And, in spite of emerging data to the contrary, evolution continues to be embraced (in fulfillment of biblical prophecy).

---

[124] See also: *"Darwin's Black Box"*; Michael Behe; *"Darwin on Trial"*; Phillip Johnson; *"Evolution: A theory I n Crisis"*; Michael Denton

> Physicists cling to their views the same way theologians do!
> **Chuck Missler**

125

History of Christian Thought and the Age of the Universe:

Christianity, for the most part, consistently taught that the earth was on the order of something less than 10,000 years based on the creation account of Genesis 1. As the scientific community began to state that the universe was much older, perhaps in the billions of years, Christian theologians went to work to see how that played with the biblical scriptures. In addition to those who remained steadfast on a "Seven Day Creation – less than 10,000 year old earth" two other areas of new basic thought emerged. One: creation days must be somehow related to ages of time rather than 24 hour days and, Two: A potential time "gap" exists between Genesis 1:1 and Genesis 1:2 in which a complete and different "age" existed on earth prior to a complete destruction and re-construction by God. Pember was an early proponent of this type of thinking stating; "We see, then that God created the heavens and the earth perfect and beautiful in their beginning, and that at some subsequent period, how remote we cannot tell, the earth had passed into a state of utter desolation, and was void of all life….For, as the fossil remains clearly show, not only were disease and death – inseparable companions of sin – then prevalent among the living creatures of the earth, but even ferocity and slaughter,. And the fact proves that these remains have nothing to do with our world; since the Bible declares that all things made by God during the Six Days were very good, and that no evil was in them till Adam sinned." [126] Even though Donald Grey Barnhouse and others continue to support "Gap" theories, the concepts are not broadly accepted and typically create more difficulties than they solve.[127] Other supporters include C.I. Scoffield. [128]

---

[125] Chuck Missler; from "Learn the Bible in 24 Hours – session #2"; see www.khouse.org

[126] Pember was an early proponent of the "Gap Theory" which is described in his book; "Earth's Earliest Ages"; G. H. Pember; Kregel Pub; initially published 1876; re-print 1975; page 34

[127] "The Invisible War" Donald Barnhouse; Zondervan Pub; copyright 1965; page 16-17

[128] "Scofield Reference Bible"; C.I Scofield; Oxford Press; copyright 1909; copyright 1967; Genesis 1:1

The idea the that the seven creation days are somehow allegorical of ages or speak of ages became the more prevalent thought as Christian thinkers tried to align scriptures with what scientists were apparently saying through out the 1900's. A great Christian defender of the faith in the mid 1900's (Bernard Ramm) was of this thought. He stated, "The majority of Christian people have believed that the world was created about 4,000 B.C, in 6 literal days. Such a view would be prompted by the simplicity of the record coupled with a complete ignorance of the data of science." [129] Peter Stoner, also a great Christian defender, wrote similar thoughts, "Genesis 1:1 does not state a time when the universe was created. As far as scriptural evidence is concerned it does not matter whether everything started five or six billion years ago, ten billion years ago, one hundred billion years ago, or any other assigned time….That the days [of Genesis] are twenty-four-hour consecutive days…This is at once ruled out by geology." [130] Indeed. Radioactive decay information developed in the 1900's clearly seemed to indicate that billions of years is a correct measure of the age of the earth.

[129] "The Christian View of Science and Scripture"; Bernard Ramm; Eerdmans Pub; copyright 1954; 6th printing 1966; page 173
[130] "Science Speaks" Peter W. Stoner; Moody Books; copyright 1958; 3rd edition 1969; page 25 & 63

As we moved towards the end of the 1900's, Christians were left with few options. Without question, real scientific data (as opposed to evolutionary thought which really only ever was a theory) indicates that the earth must be on the order of billions of years. However, these well meaning Christians, in a valiant effort to show the scriptures to be of divine origin, may have , in my opinion, "thrown the baby out with the bath water."

It should be pointed out that even though there is a body of data that supports a very old earth (billions of years) there is also a large body of data that suggest the earth is on the order of 1,000's of years. Walt Brown catalogued 34 of the key ones in his work. [131]

Christian Thinking Today:

Four basic earth age options that exist today are shown in the attached table. The first group sees the earth in billions of years but fails to recognize a creator leaving that to chance. As previously stated, this group ignores all the emerging science data like DNA failing to recognize a creator God. The second group attempts to support an old earth concept claiming consistency with scriptures but as will be shown later, this is a difficult position to take biblically. The third group attempts to demonstrate that the earth is very young which is consistent with scripture but has difficulty disproving radioactive dating associated with the billions of years apparent age. The fourth group represent only a very small number of adherents but my opinion is that this group will be dramatically growing over the coming decades. These folks see the scriptures teaching a young earth and recognize the scientific data supporting billions of year old universe but reconcile these two thoughts as consistent by the application of quantum physics. None of the first three groups has really given quantum physics merited thought which is a fatal flaw when considering something on the scale of the creation of the universe. Each of these positions will be summarized.

---

[131] "In the Beginning"; Walt Brown; ISBN 1-878026-08-9; copyright 1980; 7th Edition – 2001; page 28-35

Secular Scientists	Old Earth Creationists	Young Earth Creationists	Quantum Creationists
Earth: ~15 Billion Years	Earth: Billions of Years	Earth: < 10,000 Years	Earth: Relative
Creation Time: Big Bang	Creation Time: Ages	Creation Time: 7 days	Creation Time: 7days and 15 billion years
Creator: None	Creator: God of Bible	Creator: God of Bible	Creator: God of Bible
Science data supports old earth	Science data supports old earth	Science data supports young earth	Science data supports old earth and young earth
Science data does not support random evolution vs creator	Science data supports creator	Science data supports creator	Science data supports creator
	Bible's support for old earth is debatable	Bible "prima facia" strong support for young earth	Bible "prima facia" strong support for young earth
Ignores quantum physics	Ignores quantum physics	Ignores quantum physics	Uses quantum physics physics to explain old vs young dichotomy

Old Earth Creationists:

There is a substantial group of well-respected Christian Theologians who have an "Old Earth" view. For this reason, it should not be quickly dismissed as inconsistent with scripture. Dr. Norman Geisler is a very well respected Christian thinker of our time who currently serves as President of Southern Evangelical Seminary in Charlotte, North Carolina. Geisler makes some strong points that an old earth is consistent with scriptures. He states that. "Indeed, since the Bible does not say exactly how old the universe is, the ages of the earth is not a test for orthodoxy. In fact, many orthodox evangelical scholars hold the universe is millions or billions of years old, including Augustine, Warfield, John Walvoord, Fransis Schaeffer...." [132] This point is reinforced in his theological series stating again, "The age of the earth is not a test for orthodoxy....The *fact* of Creations (vs. evolution) is more important than the

---

time of Creation." [133]   Two additional credible Christian creationists representing similar thoughts are Boa and Bowman. They state "The scientific evidence solidly shows, however, that the Earth has had an oxidizing atmosphere for about four billion years." [134] In light of these great thinkers, we as Christians still are plagued with a gnawing thought in the background. If the bible is the "Words of God", we would naturally take them at pretty much face value, assuming that: "God means what He says and says what He means." [135] We are thereby faced with a real difficulty. Geisler himself really says it well, "The problem is deepened by the fact that there is *prima facie* evidence to indicate that he days of Genesis 1 are indeed twenty-four-hour periods." [136]

Young Earth Creationists:

It is this *"prima facie"* evidence that drives many Christians to continue to defend a younger earth. Does Genesis 1 really clearly state 7 days or can it be inferred to mean something different? Hebrew scholars typically take a strong and consistent stand in this matter which can be seen in Dr. Bernard Northrup statements, "Probably, so far as I know, there is no professor of Hebrew or Old Testament at any world-class university who does not believe that the writer of Genesis 1-11 intended to convey to their readers the ideas that creation took place in a series of six days which were the same as the days of 24 hours we now experience." [137] There are several good Christian scholars who support a young earth and seven days of creation. Included are the "Answers in Genesis" organization who state, "Being really honest, you would have to admit that you could never get the idea of millions of years from reading this passage [Genesis 1]." [138]   Dr. Henry Morris of the Institute for Creation Research also supports young earth concepts. Some of his thoughts include the idea that the universe was created with the appearance of age, which can

---

[133] "Systematic Theology – Vol II – God and Creation"; Dr. Norman Geisler; Bethany House; copyright 2003; page 471

[134] "20 Compelling Evidences that God Exists"; Kenneth Doa and Robert Bowman; River Oak Pub; copyright 2002; page 87

[135] Phrase used often by Dr. Chuck Missler in reference to appropriate hermeneutics (interpreting the bible); "The Book of Revelation"; Dr. Chuck Missler; Koinonia House Pub; copyright 2005; page 7

[136] "Baker – Encyclopedia of Christian Apologetics"; Geisler; page 270

[137] Dr. Northrup from a tape of his lecture at the ICC conference in Pittsburgh, 1994, as quoted in "Notes in Genesis Chapter One" Lambert Dolphin; http://ldolphin.org/genesis1.html; page 16/17

[138] "Answers Book"; Don Batten editor with Ken Ham, Sarfati, Wieland; Master Books; copyright 1990; revised 2000; 29th printing Feb 2004; page 33

potentially explain light from stars millions of light years away.[139] Another popular book supporting a seven day creation was put together with the explicit intent of supporting this idea. This book is a compilation of short articles by 50 different scientists and engineers who all support a 7 day creation approach. These thoughts are summarized by Ashton, the editor as, "Having reviewed the discussions posed by these scientists, in the light of my own education and experience, I am convinced that a literal understanding of the Genesis account of creation is the most reasonable explanation out of all the current theories of how we came to be here." [140]

How clearly does the Bible State a Six-Day Creation?

The Bibles position on a six-day creation (7th day being the day of rest) account is supported in three areas. The first is Genesis 1 itself which as stated above, all Hebrew scholars will tell us that this is 6 twenty four hours periods of time. Second is an account in Exodus 20 where God literally and verbally spoke with the children of Israel telling them that he made the heavens and the earth in 6 days (Ex 20:11) (this is only one of about three times when people actually heard the voice of God). The third is the astounding fact that the only portion of scripture (10 verses out of over 31,000 in the bible) that was literally written by God, the finger of God, poking through the fabric of space and time, etching out a tablet, God chose to reaffirm the fact He made the heavens and the earth in 6 days (Ex 31:17-18).

Enter – Quantum Physics:

Quantum physics foundations were laid in 1900-1926 time period with Max Planck's work of black body radiation being an initial step. Quantum mechanic concepts are difficult to grasp and shock us at the very level of fundamental understanding of the universe. As tough as these things are, we find estimates that "30 percent of the U.S. gross national product is based on inventions made possible by quantum mechanics, from semiconductor in computer chips to lasers in compact-disc players, magnetic resonance imaging in hospitals, and much more." [141] For the purposes of understanding the concept of time and age of the universe a few things are worth pointing out. Albert Einstein developed theories on time and relativity. Of keynote, is that time is variable in our time-space continuum that we are a part of. Time is not

---

[139] "The Genesis Flood"; John Whitcomb and Henry Morris; P&R Pub; copyright 1961; page 345

[140] "In Six Days"; John Ashton PhD; Master Books; copyright 2000; 4th printing Sept 2003; page 6

[141] "100 Years of Quantum Mysteries" Max Tegmark and John Wheeler; Scientific American; Feb. 2004; page 69

a constant in spite of our normal thinking that it is. Time varies with gravitation and speed. Time relativity has been proven many times but two experiments are worth noting. [142] One is an experiment done in 1971 with cesium-beam clocks sent on round the world trips. These highly accurate clocks were loaded on commercial aircraft and flown in different directions around the world. Because one went with the earth's rotation and the second went against the earth's rotation, they had different true velocities. Because of the differences in velocity, they experienced different "times" and when the clocks were matched up, it turns out that the difference in time was exactly what was predicted. A second example is the two international standard clocks. One in near sea level (80 ft.) in Greenwich England and the second is at 5,400-ft altitude in Bolder, Colorado. Because the Denver clock is at a higher altitude, it is in a lower gravitational field. Theory of relativity states that time is faster in a low gravitational field and slower in a high gravitational field. And, as predicted, the Greenwich clock runs 5 microseconds slower every year as a result of this higher gravitational field.

A hypothetical problem is posed about an astronaut heading towards a high gravitational black hole, which illustrates how leveraging gravity is on the effect of time. If an astronaut can be seeing as he is traveling through space by observers on the earth and vise-versa the astronaut can look back and observe earth we will

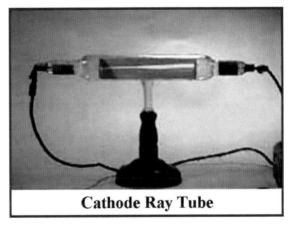

Cathode Ray Tube

illustrated the principle of time relativity. Initially in the trip we watch the astronaut and see him doing things in the space ship at normal speed. He like wise will observe activity on the earth as normal. As the astronaut gets closer and closer to the high gravitational black hole, he begins to see activity on the earth as speeding up. In fact, the closer he gets to the black hole, he will observe life on earth turning into a complete blur of extremely high speed activity. Conversely, we on earth see the astronaut appear to be operating in slow motion, slowing down more and more as he approaches the black hole. In fact, as he gets close, it would appear to us on earth that the astronaut had

---

[142] "Stretching the Heavens"; Chuck Missler; Khouse;
http://khouse.org/aritcles/technicles/19990701-245.html

basically frozen in place with not appreciable movement. This problem illustrates the fact that gravity is a significant factor on experiencing time. It further illustrates that we are not all going through time together. Yes, here on earth it is nearly imperceptible between people living at high altitude for example over those living at sea level, but if you are dealing with large differences in gravitational fields, time clearly distorts on a large scale.

Creation and Quantum Physics:

There are a small group of thinkers who are applying quantum physics to the formation of the universe to better understand the creation event. Gerald Schroeder Ph.D. has a great work called "Genesis and the Big Bang." He is a nuclear physics and pioneer in this area. Schroeder sees that location during an event of the magnitude of the formation of the universe has a dramatic effect on time experienced. Working with a universe development model that starts with the entire universe initially at some 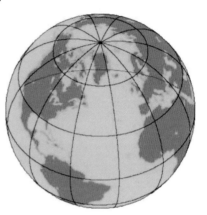 specific point in space and then expanding the complete universe from that center point, which is consistent with most secular science "big bang" type concepts, Schroeder ends up with some dramatic results. Time experienced by someone who was traveling with the matter that went to the outer edges of the universe would have experienced something like 15 billion years while the person located at the center of the universe during the expansion would have experienced something like 6 days. For this reason, he sees consistency between a 6 day creation and a 15 billion year **at the same time**. Both are true. "Both are. Literally! With no allegorical modifications of these two simultaneous, yet different, time periods…because the same single sequence of events that encompasses the time period from "the beginning" to the appearance of mankind did take six days and 15 billion years – simultaneously – starting at the same instant and finishing at the same instant." [143] This difference is known as "time dilation." "The difference in perceived time is called relativistic time dilation, the dilation that makes the first six days of Genesis reassuringly compatible with the 15 billion years of cosmology." [144] Schroeder additionally points out that there are time issues associated with the

---

[143] "Genesis and the Big Bang"; Gerald Schroeder Ph.D.; Bantam Books; copyright 1990; page 29
[144] Ibid; page 44

physical state of the universe during its formation as well, "based on the stretching of space has on the perception of distant information…and the location of the perception is not from a particular point is space but rather from a particular moment in time, the time at which energy and quarks confined into the stable matter, that is, protons." [145]   Part of the point here is that time measurements are strongly affected by the state of the universe at the moment the question is asked.

It is provocative that you can take the current estimated size of the universe, define its "expansion factor" and integrate that into the estimate age of the universe into the outer boundary, the result for the age at the center is surprisingly small.   Doing the math: the estimated expansion factor of the universe at its formation, based on its current estimated size is 10^{12};   The estimated age of the universe is 16 billion years = 16 billion x 365 days per year = 6×10^{12} days; 6×10^{12} days / 10^{12} expansion = 6 days. Provocative!

Another physicist working in this area is D. Russell Humphreys, Ph.D. He has developed a scenario that is consistent will all quantum physics models called a "white hole" which is simplistically speaking a black hole in reverse. If you take this approach as the creation event, where, rather than a black hole which has great mass and is pulling everything in, increasing the mass, we start will all the mass located at and single point and expand it out. The results are similar to above in that as the event horizon moves from the outer edges of space towards the center where all the mass was originally prior to expansion, mass traveling to the outer edges would experience something on the order of 15 billion years while mass remaining near the center would experience something like 6 days. [146]

Another different approach but related part of quantum physics is Barry Setterfield's work on the changing of the speed of light.   We all view the speed of light as a constant although we don't know this for sure. Setterfield first announced his thoughts in 1987 and although very controversial, some secular physicists have begun to publish in this area (see Albrich and McGuire – Feb 1998). Setterfield makes initial claim using speed of light measurements over the past 300 years (160 measurements in total) that light could have possibly slowed by a factor of 2.54×10^{10} over what it is today. What does this mean to us? Many other properties are linked with the speed of light and if these results prove valid, we will discover that radioactive dating and many

---

[145] see; geraldschroeder.com/age.html

[146] "Starlight and Time"; D.Russell Humphreys, Ph.D.; Master Books; copyright 1994; 7th printing Mar 2002; page 29

other factors will dramatically change. Setterfield correlates this data to conclude that 15 billion years is also consistent with a 6-day creation account.
[147]

Summary

Most importantly, if you are having a discussion with anyone about the age of the universe, and the conversation is not in terms of the theory of relativity, you are wasting you time. Time, is clearly proven to be relative, and when dealing with a problem the size of the creation of the universe, it is without a doubt a significant factor. Time is strongly affected or determined by location and position. To answer the question of how old the universe is, you must first ask; "Where are you standing?" The bible has clearly stated the universe had a beginning (confirmed by physics in the last 100 years), time started with that beginning (confirmed by physics) and at some location within the universe during the creation event a time of 6 days was experienced (to be confirmed by quantum physics). Our understanding of quantum physics is still very sketchy and is being constantly refined today. It's concepts impact what we understand at such a high level, Neils Bohr (one of the early founders of quantum physics) stated, "anyone who is not shocked by quantum physics, clearly doesn't understand it." The bible on the other hand, has been demonstrating for thousands of years that it contains information well beyond the capacity of it's writers, indicating without a doubt that it is the words of God from outside out time-space continuum.

> **"Anyone who isn't shocked by quantum physics, clearly doesn't understand it."**
> **Neils Bohr**

---

[147] Several of Setterfields articles can be found on Lambert Dolphins website: www.ldolphin.org

Realizing the difficulties associate with time dilation, Albert Einstein said:

> **"People like us who believe in physics, know that the distinction between the past, present and the future is only a stubbornly persistent illusion."**
>
> **Albert Einstein**

Chuck Missler : "One of the many advantages that 20th century science has given us is that, thanks to Dr. Albert Einstein's brilliant discoveries, we now know that time is a physical property and is subject to mass, acceleration, and gravity. We have come to realize that we live in a four-dimensional continuum properly known as "space-time." (This is what Paul seems to imply in his letter to the Ephesians 3:18) It is interesting that when one takes the apparent 10^{12} expansion factor involved in the theories of the "expanding universe," that an assumed 16 billion years reduce to six days!" [148]

---

[148] http://www.khouse.org/articles/2003/492/

5 – Astronomy and Cosmology

Chapter 5.3

All Matter is Actively Held Together by God

Colossians 1:16-17
*"For by Him [beloved Son – Jesus] all things were created, both in the heavens and on earth, visible and invisible, whether thrones or dominions or rulers or authorities – all things have been created through Him and for Him. He is before all things, **and in Him all things hold together**."* (NAS)

Jesus, our Lord, is actively holding the universe (all things) together!

Hold Together (Greek - *sunistano*); definition – to commend, establish, stand near, consist; Strong's #4921

Wow! You know our Lord Jesus created the entire universe? Not only everything we see, but the things we don't see. Think that is pretty good? Well, check this out. Not only did He create everything, He is holding it together! That means, dear friends, that Christ is actively involved at the atomic level! It may come as a surprise to you to understand that the physicists don't fully understand the atomic forces of the universe. As best as we understand it, there are four basic forces, each quite different in the way they operate:

Force	Relative Strength	Distance	What does it do?
Strong Force	$1.7 \; 10^{38}$	Diameter of the Nucleus	Holds the Nucleus of an atom together
Electro Magnetic Force	$1.2 \; 10^{36}$	Infinite range	Holds together atoms and molecules
Weak Force	$1.7 \; 10^{32}$	0.1% of a diameter of a Proton	
Gravity	1	Infinite range	Acts on large bodies

Atomic Forces of the Universe

A Nucleus of an atom contains protons and neutrons. Protons are positively charged particles. According to "Electro Magnetic Forces," opposite charged particles attract (a positive and a negative) but like charged particles (a positive and a positive or a negative and a negative) repel each other. Protons in the nucleus are positively charged and should therefore naturally repel each other and all atomic nucleuses should "fly apart." Why doesn't this happen? Well, it is because there is a substantially stronger force called the "Strong Force" which pulls the Protons together. Well, if that is true, why doesn't all matter pull together into a giant lump. That is because the "Strong Force," although more that 100 times greater than the "Electro Magnetic Force," only acts over a very short distance. In fact, it only operates over the distance of the nucleus itself. At least, that is what today's physics is teaching.

Irrespective of the fact that we struggle to understand all this, scripture informs us that Jesus is an active participant in "holding" all this together. Again, I say Wow! All this kind of begs the question; "Will He ever let go?" For that answer, see the next chapter.

> ## "There are no maverick molecules out there doing their own thing!"
> ## M. Connelly

[149]

---

[149] Mark Connelly - Stated during a message on the bigness of Jesus on 12/3/06 at Superstition Springs Community Church – Gilbert Arizona

Chapter 5.4

Release of Atomic Particles

2 Peter 3:6-7 See also 2 Peter 3:12; Jude 7 and Genesis 9:8-17
"*...through which the world at that time was destroyed, being flooded with water. But **by His word the present heavens and earth are being reserved for fire, kept for the day of judgment** and destruction of ungodly men.*" (NAS)

The day will come when the earth and the universe will be destroyed by fire, like the flood of Noah.

Reserved (Greek - *tereo*); definition – to watch over, to guard Strong's #5083
Fire (Greek - *pur*); definition – fire; Strong's #4442

As we saw in the last chapter, there are some pretty strong forces operating in the atom. Why is an atom bomb so powerful. Well, basically, when a neutron particle is shot into an atom, which subsequently splits, setting off a chain reaction by sending off more neutrons to split more atoms; the restraining forces are broken and a huge amount of energy (the energy that was holding

the atom together) is released, basically in the form of heat. This is the definition of "Atomic Fission." We are talking a lot of energy. That is why a small atomic bomb can destroy a major city, the results of Atomic Fission.

2 Peter 3:12 indicates that the universe will "*be destroyed by burning and the **elements will melt** with intense heat.*" Elements is from the Greek word Stoicheion (Strongs #4747) which is the word from which we get Stoichiometry as in "Stoichiometric Table" which is the table of elements. This is a shocking revelation when we realize that scripture, 1,800 years before

the discovery of the atom describes accurately the intense heat resulting from the release of atoms.

If Jesus is "holding the universe together" will He ever relax His grip? Will he let things fly apart and therefore cause a huge release of heat energy? Well, if you read our covenant with God established at the time of Noah very carefully, read the fine print, we are heading for another world wide disaster. This covenant, recorded in Genesis 9 provides us with the assurance that God will never again destroy the earth and all flesh "BY WATER." Does that mean He won't destroy all life again? Nope! In fact it implies that there will be another destruction, only not by water as in the flood of Noah. The Holy Spirit, in 2 Peter 3:6-7, instructs us that the present "heavens and earth" are being reserved for fire. Jude 7 also alludes to judgment but goes further to describe "eternal fire."

Chapter 5.5

Fabric of Space

Isaiah 34:4
"And all the host of __heaven will wear away__, and the __sky [heaven] will be rolled up lake a scroll__..." (NAS)

Our universe displays some shocking properties; it can be stretched, rolled up, torn, worn out, shaken, split up, burnt up and split apart! To be "rolled up" that must mean in one dimension, it must be fairly thin.

To us, the universe is so large, we can't imagine things like "rolling up" or "tearing" being able to happen to it. God gives us insight, which confirms His power and control of the universe as a whole, which also provides us with future insight as to what will happen to the universe. Tabulated below is some of the unusual properties that our universe exhibits.

Biblical Properties of the Universe	
Stretching the Heavens	2Sam 22:10; Job 9:8; 26:7; 37:18; Ps 18:9; 104:2; 144:5; Isa 40:22; 42:5: 45:12; 48:13; 51:13; Jer 10:12; 51:15; Eze 1:22; Zech 12:1
Torn	Isa 64:1; Heb 1:11-12
Worn out like a garment	Psalm 102:25; Isa 34:4
Shaken	Hag 2:21; Hag 2:6; Isa 13:13
Burnt up	2 Pet 3:12
Split apart like a scroll	Rev 6:14 (Sky)
Rolled up like a mantel or scroll	Heb 1:12; Isa 34:4 (Sky)

Amazing 4 D properties of the Universe

5 – Astronomy and Cosmology

- Heavens (Hebrew - *Shamayim*); #8064 –Heaven, sky - to be lofty; the sky (as aloft; the dual perhaps alluding to the visible arch in which the clouds move, as well as to the higher ether where the celestial bodies revolve):
- Heavens (Greek – *Ouranos*); #3772 - the sky; by extension, heaven (as the abode of God)
- Rend (Tear) (Hebrew – *qara*); #7167 – to tear
- Become Old (Worn Out) (Greek – *palaioo*); #3822 - to make (passively, become) worn out, or declare obsolete: [decay]
- Wear Out (Hebrew – *Balah*) #1086 - to fail; by implication to wear out, decay
- Wear Away (Hebrew – *maqaq*) #4743 – to decay, rot, fester, pine away:
- Roll Up (Greek – *helisso*); #1667 – to roll up or to coil or wrap:
- Roll Up (Hebrew – *galal*) #1556 – to roll, roll away
- Shake (Hebrew – *raash*); #7493 – to quake, shake;
- Tremble / Shake (Hebrew – *ragaz*) #7264 – to be agitated, quiver, quake, be excited, perturbed:
- Burnt Up (on fire) (Greek – *puroo*) #4448 – to set on fire, to burn
- Split Apart (Greek – *apochorizo*) #673 – to separate, part asunder: (Rev 6:14 – as a scroll rolled up)

As we envision the universe to be more that just the 3 dimensions we typically think, and see it in its 4+ dimensional light, we find that in at least one of the dimensions, the universe is basically "thin." This is brought to light when we talk of the "Fabric of Space." Although man has only come to understand this in the last 100 years, since Einstein, the Scriptures have indicated this all along. In fact, the bible has revealed some shocking characteristics that we would not normally consider in our universe:

Rolled Up: as the universe is "thin" in one dimension, God tells us it will one day be "rolled up." Wow!

Shaken: God, who is outside our universe, has the ability to and will "shake it."

Worn Out: this is a confirmation of the 2nd and 3rd laws of thermodynamics. The 2nd law states that as energy is being used, the universe is wearing down and the 3rd law states that things are "breaking down" and becoming less ordered.

Burnt Up: in a shocking description of atomic fission (2 Peter 3:12) we find that the heavens are being reserved for a 2nd judgment (the 1st earth wide judgment being that of Noah and the flood). For additional information see section 4.6 on Judgments and 5.4.5 on Atomic Fission

Split Apart and Torn: This can only happen if the universe is "thin" is some dimension

Secular scientists are in general agreement today that the universe is basically "flat." Although we don't know for sure, there are 3 possibilities for the "shape" of our universe and this is a subject of primary study. One of the key objectives of the Microwave Anisotropy Probe (MAP) satellite mission (see picture), launched by the US on June30, 2001 and was to make measurements to help determine the shape of the universe. Based on the initial data from the satellite which is still operating (it was planed as a 2 year prime mission but due to conservative design and judicious use of energy, the mission is now extended to Sept 2009) most scientists conclude that the universe is "flat." MAP Scientists: "We now know that the universe is flat with only a 2% margin of error." [150] That's pretty flat.

WMAP satellite probe leaving earth's orbit

The 3 possible shapes of the universe are envisioned because of three possible curvatures. As shown in the figure: if the curvature is positive, then space would be shaped like a sphere (just the surface – it would be "hollow" on the inside); if the curvature is negative, then space would be "saddle" shaped; if the curvature is 1, or in essence, no curvature, the universe would be basically flat. Because the universe is apparently isotropic or homogeneous on a large

---

[150] MAP or WMAP web site is http://map.gsfc.nasa.gov/index.html

scale, it is generally believed that the "flat" universe is the best model. This view may change in the future but we have confidence from the scriptures that independent of the shape, in some dimension the universe is thin and therefore can be subjected to the various scenarios that God has described.

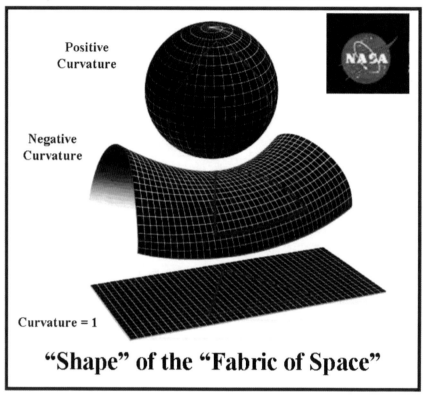

"Shape" of the "Fabric of Space"

	Heavens	Rend / Torn	
Isa 64:1	#8064	#7167	
	Shamayim	*Qara*	
	Heavens	Worn Out	Roll Up
Heb 1:11-12	#3772	#3822	#1667
	Ouranos	*Palaioo*	*Helisso*
	Heavens	Wear Out	Perish
Psalm 102:25	#8064	#1086	#6
	Shamayim	*Balah*	Abad
	Heavens	Shake	
Hag 2:21	#8064	#7493	
	Shamayim	*Raash*	
	Heavens	Shake	
Hag 2:6	#8064	#7493	
	Shamayim	*Raash*	
	Heavens	Tremble / Shake	
Isa 13:13	#8064	#7264	
	Shamayim	*Ragaz*	
	Heavens	Burnt Up	
2 Peter 3:12	#3772	#4448	
	Ouranos	*Purpo*	
	Heavens/Sky	Split Apart	
Rev 6:14	#3772	#673	
	Ouranos	*Apochorizo*	
	Heavens	Wear Away	Roll Up
Isa 34:4	#8064	#4743	#1556
	Shamayim	*Maqaq*	*Galal*

Table showing properties of the universe and the scriptural words with Strong's reference numbers for further study.

5 – Astronomy and Cosmology

Chapter 5.6

360 Day Year and Earth's Cosmic Catastrophes

Genesis 7:11 & 8:3-4

"...*in the **second month, on the seventeenth day of the month**, on the same day all the fountains of the great deep burst open...and at the end of **one hundred and fifty days** the water decreased. In the **seventh month, on the seventeenth day of the month**, the ark rested...*" (NAS) [5 months – 150 days]

God's dealing with the earth has included some incredible global catastrophes brought on by cosmic disturbances orchestrated by the Hand of God.

Catastrophism

In one sense, this is an outrageous claim, one typically not supported by most of today's scientists, secular or of faith. The prevailing thought is that our universe and planet has existed for billions of years, and during this time, the world as we know it has slowly taken shape. Mountains have been put in place, rivers have cut deep canyons and the ocean has defined the shoreline. Plenty of stable and consistent time has passed and enabled life on this planet to develop into what we see today. This concept is known as Uniformism. Uniformism is a key tenant in evolution, providing the long time periods thought necessary to form and develop life. At least, this is what is surmised. Catastrophism is a thought that the earth and universe that we see today has been dramatically shaped and formed by cosmic catastrophic events. Catastrophism is typically denied by the Uniformists and in a sense, there are few followers but they are comprised of both secular and those of faith. If these claims of catastrophists are true, what data can be provided to validate it? Does the bible have anything to add to the subject? Surprisingly the bible has a great deal to say about some significant cosmic events that have occurred through the course of biblical history.

- 1st We will start with one key but very shocking fact that I believe is undeniable which forces us to seriously consider a catastrophic approach
- 2nd we will propose some theories as to the physical origin of the catastrophes
- 3rd we will examine the biblical record to see if there are any supporting accounts
- 4th look closely at some descriptions from eye witnesses
- 5th we will look into prophecy and see what quite possibility we all might be facing in the future. Strap in, it is going to be a bumpy ride as we will challenge your perceptions of the universe. You will never look at the stars and planets the same again.

360 Day Year?

Reading some biblical passages that had references to days and months have always been perplexing to me until one day, when I read something that blew the socks off my feet. What I read was that all ancient civilizations had a 360 day year. I vaguely remembered some things from ancient history classes in High School but it was passed off back then as simply, primitive people didn't understand. When I read that ALL ancient civilizations had a 360 day year, and then read that the bible used a 360 day year I was blown away. How could this be? Everyone should know that there is something like 365 ¼ days in a year!

Immanuel Velikovsky, a catastrophist of the early 20th century catalogues 12 of the key ancient civilizations (see table below), around the globe demonstrating they all had a 360 day year, comprised of 12 months of 30 days each. [151] Let that sink in for a minute. Every person on the planet up to about 700 BC was tracking a 30 day month, matching a lunar cycle with 12 cycles in each month. Babylonians serve as a good example. They divided most all mathematics into this cycle. We find that they were the ones who established the 360 degrees of a circle, built they wall around Babylon as 360 furlongs in length and established the 12 signs of the starts, one for each month with each month being divided into 3 decans. [152] Did the earth really only have 360 days in the year? Perhaps the ancients just "rounded off" their numbering system to keep things simple; at least I have heard that as a suggestion. This thought quickly breaks down as you consider that in a mere short span of 36 years, the summer

---

[151] "Worlds in Collision"; Immanuel Velikovsky; Doubleday & Company Inc; Garden City, NY; Copyright 1950; 6th printing 1950; Chapter 8 page 330-359
[152] "Worlds in Collision"; Immanuel Velikovsky; page 333

and winter cycles would have been completely flipped. Consider also that the Pre-Druids of Great Britain constructed Stonehenge around 1800 BC for the probable purpose of tracking the stars. This monumental feat, one which we have difficulty determining how they accomplished, included as example: transporting stone 56, which weighs over 50 tons, from a quarry over 300 miles away to its current location, being transported over land, water then land again. Design and construction was not accomplished by a primitive folk, it was a masterpiece of astronomy, engineering and mathematics. It strikes me as odd that these people would have "rounded off" over 5 days of the year.

Velikovsky: "All over the world we find that there was at some time the same calendar of 360 days, and that at some later date, about the 7th century before the present era, 5 days were added at the end of the year, as "days over the year," or "days of nothing.""[153] This data strongly suggests that the ancient world turned about its axis and rotated about the sun in a fashion that resulted in only 360 days.

India	12 months - 30 days	Egyptian	12 months - 30 days
Persia	12 months - 30 days	Greece	12 months - 30 days
Babylonian	12 months - 30 days	Mayan	12 months - 30 days
Assyrians	12 months - 30 days	Peru	12 months - 30 days
Israelites	12 months - 30 days	China	12 months - 30 days
Roman	12 months - 30 days	Mexicans	12 months - 30 days

Ancient civilizations with a 360 day year

Does the bible support this shocking claim? Consider the following. We find several references to days, years and months and all of them are based on a 360 day year. Lets look at the two primary ones:

- Flood of Noah – We find in Genesis 7:11 that the flood began on the 17th day of the 2nd month of the year. Genesis 8:3-4 tells us that the flood did not abate until the 17th day of the 7th month and defines the interval in Gen 8:3 as a period of 150 days. This equates to 5 months of exactly 30 days.
- Duration of the "Times of Jacobs Trouble" – In biblical prophecy, there is a defining key timeframe of 7 years commonly referred to as the "Tribulation." The last half of this period is going to be very

---

[153] "Worlds in Collision"; Immanuel Velikovsky; page 341

intense and will be 3 ½ years in duration. Daniel the prophet, clearly indicates in Daniel 9:27 that this is a period of 3 ½ years [middle of a "week" which is a "week of years" or 7 years – the middle then being 3 ½ years]. He defines the start of this period (one of great calamity "*a time of distress such as never occurred since there was a nation until that time*" Dan 12:1b) as starting at a very identifiable event. That event is the "Abomination of Desolation" (Dan 12:11) in which the "Antichrist" will enter the Holy of Holies of the Jewish temple and sacrificing a pig on the sacred altar thereby desecrating the entire Temple. Jesus refers to this events in His end times prophecy (Matt 24:15) and we all find it described in Revelation. Revelation clearly states this last half of the tribulation as a 42 month period (Rev 11:2 & 13:5) and also makes reference to it as 1,260 days (which equates to 42 months of exactly 30 days for those who don't have a calculator handy) (Rev 11:3 & 12:6 see also Rev 12:14 linked with Dan 7:25 & Dan 12:7).

- Others include: Ester 1:4 (days of Ahasuerus stated as180 implied as a half year or 6 months;   Days of morning defined as 1 month and equated to 30 days (Deut 34:8; 21:13; Numb 20:29

"We refuse to surrender Holy Writ to the tender mercies of those who approach it with the ignorance of pagans and the animus of apostates" Sir R. Anderson

---

Sir Robert Anderson who was head of the English famed Scotland Yard highlighted the fact of the biblical 360 day year and showed how it was pivotal to understanding prophecy. He meticulously tracked Daniel's prophecy of the coming messiah and shows how Jesus, the Christ, completely fulfilled these accurate prophecies when He entered Jerusalem on the exact day as predicted by Daniel over 500 years before hand (See Daniel 9:24-27). Shockingly, we find that these prophecies were intended to be literal and accurate by Jesus' statements of the time. Jesus held the Jews accountable for not recognizing the day (not times) of His coming. On the day of Jesus' triumphal entry, as He came to Jerusalem in fulfillment of biblical prophecy to present Himself as the "Messiah', He predicts the destruction of Jerusalem because they failed to recognize "this thy day" (Luke 19:41) the day promised by God that the Messiah would appear (as revealed by Daniel in Dan 9:24-27). Jesus' prophecy of destruction comes to pass in 70 AD when Titus Vespesian and the

Roman armies finally broke through the city wall, ending the siege and destroying some 2 million people. Use of the 360 day "ancient year" or "prophetic year" as Anderson refers to it gets you to the exact date of Jesus' arrival. Anderson: "It follows therefore that the prophetic year is not the Julian year, but the ancient year of 360 days." [154] Anderson's book "The Prince that Shall Come" is a classic providing one of the most credible accounting of the exact dates of Daniel's prophecy was written in 1884 and available today in reprint. [155]

Conjecture for what caused the shift from 360 to 360+ days

One fascinating theory has been proposed by three men who work together developing an orbital mechanics model that provides accurate predictions of several catastrophes documented in the bible. Donald Patten (Geography – History), Ronald Hatch (orbital mechanics) and Dr. Loren Steinhauer (astronautics – orbital mechanics) collaborated on several works including "The Long Day of Joshua and Six other Catastrophes". [156] They propose that Mars and Earths orbits were different in ancient times and there was an overlapping region which resulted in these two planets crossing paths. What their analytical model shows is a pattern of close "fly by's" occurring in a 54 year and multiples there of cycles. Astoundingly, a close flyby occurs every 108 years which would result in dramatic effects on the earth. But wait, there is more; Patten shows that of the 11 possible 108 year close "fly by's" the bible documents catastrophes in 8 of those scenarios! Wow! The last close "fly by" occurs during the time of Isaiah on March 20/21, 701 BC and is so close that it results in altering the orbits of both Earth and Mars into what they are today changing Earth's year from 360 to the 365+ days.

---

[154] "The Coming Prince"; Sir Robert Anderson; page 75

[155] Sir Robert Anderson, "The Coming Prince"; originally published in 1884; Kregel Publications, Grand Rapids MI; 19th edition 1975

[156] "The Long Day of Joshua and Six Other Catastrophes"; Donald W. Patten, Ronald Hatch, and Dr. Loren Steinhauer; Pacific Meridian Pub; Seattle, Washington 98125; Copyright 1973

5 – Astronomy and Cosmology

Date	Size	Date	Event	Reference
2362	⎫		Noah's Flood	
2254	⎭		?	
2146	○			
2038			?	
1930	●	October 25.	Tower of Babel	
1877	●	March 20/21	Sodom and Gomorrah	
1771			?	
1663	○		Job	Job 1:16; Job 26, 38, 41
1555				
1447	●	March 20/21	Exodus of Israel from Egypt	
1404	●	October 25.	Joshua's Long Day	Joshua 10:11
1296			?	
1188	○	October 25.	Deborah Debacle	Judges 5:20
1080	○	October 25.	Samuelic Catastrophe	1 Sam 7:10
1025	○		Lesser Davidic (speculative)	2 Sam 22:8-19; Psalm 18:7-18
972	○	October 25.	Greater Davidic Catastrophe	1 Chr 21:14-16; 2 Sam 24:15-16; 1 Kings 5:5
864	○	October 25.	Elijahic Catastrophe	1 Kings 18:28; (referenced by Isa 9:1)
756	●	October 25.	Joel Amos Catastrophe	
701	●	March 20/21	Isaiahic Catastrophe	

Table of Biblical Catastrophes showing 54 and 108 year cycles

Pattten et all's orbital model shows close "flyby's" occurring on either October 25/31 or March 20/21 of the close flyby or resonance years. [157] Answered by this theory is the perplexing preoccupation that ancient civilizations had in tracking the movements of the planets: there confusing desire to worship or make gods of the planets; and the link with cyclic catastrophes recorded in the scriptures.

[157] See summary in "The Long Day of Joshua"; pages 4-5 and 273

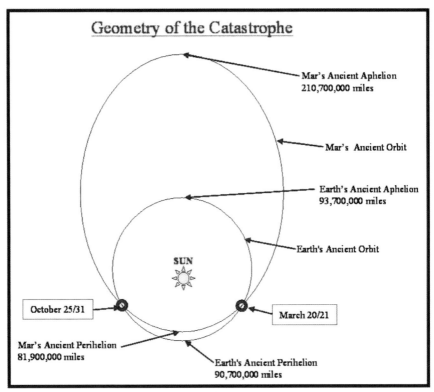

Patten's Orbital Model for Earth and Mars Ancient Orbits

What would be the effects of such a close "fly by" here on Earth? Key effects are summarized below: (see page 108 of reference book and other pages as noted)

- Bolides and Meteors (fire and brimstone); documented in the 701 BC event. Likely result from asteroids around Mars and would have impacted both the Earth and the Moon (as we see current evidences on both planets) (page 92)

- Tidal Waves; Massive tidal waves (swells of over 50 feet) would result. Page 111 covers this. It is noted that one of the original Roman capital cities was on the coast of what is today Italy but was swept away by a tidal flood in 701 BC. The capital was then moved to its current location significantly inland (15 miles) at Rome (page15). A similar effect on Mars would have occurred to its crust. The deep rifts that are currently seen currently evidence this. One is documented at 10 miles deep and 2,800 miles long (page 113)

- Atmospheric noise; Earth's magnetic field is 240,000 miles in distance (beyond the moon) and a fly through by Mars would have created loud and terrible exchanges of static electricity between the planets. The noise is documented in the ancient occurrences (page 113)
- Spin axis shifts; a change in the spin axis of both the earth and Mars would be experienced. This could result in a temporary "wobble" of the earth. (page 126)
- Reversal of the earth's magnetic field; This has been validated by geologist of today (page 109)
- Earthquakes; Documented in several of the catastrophes (page 142)

Although a conjecture the Mars fly by, it is a very provocative concept explaining how the Earth was changed from the 360 day orbit. Whether it was Mars or some other cosmic disturbance we are not sure but Patten poses a very well defended option that is in sync with biblical accounts.

Biblical Accounts of a Catastrophe

An example of a catastrophe and the last one to occur causing the change in the earths orbit was in the time of Isaiah and King Hezekiah in 701 BC. The Assyrians have ruthlessly been taking over the nations, conquering the earth when they set their sights on Israel. In fulfillment of prophecy because of their disobedience, God brings the Assyrians in and they conquer the  Northern Tribes of Israel. Later, they come against the Southern Tribes of Judah. Most of Judah is conquered and Jerusalem becomes the single holdout. Hezekiah is king at the time and has been following the advice, contrary to God's direction, of his counselor to attempt to ally with Egypt for money for protection. The mighty Assyrian horde, who were noted for their ruthless and relentless style of overrunning and conquering nations came against Jerusalem in siege. A siege was a devastating thing in ancient times. A city was basically surrounded and then contained and left to starve being they had no food supplies. Often, sieges would go for 1-2 years resulting in shocking behavior as the citizens attempted to survive without means such as cannibalism which was a common result near the end of a siege. In this situation, Hezekiah eventually turns from the bad advise of his counselors and decides to turn to God for help. He goes to the Lord in prayer and calls the entire city to follow. God hears his prayers and the blasphemous statements of the Assyrians and intervenes. That night, God sends and angel into the Assyrian camp who destroys 185,000 Assyrian soldiers, completely devastating the army. The few who remain are forced to withdraw and return to Assyria in defeat. The account is recorded in 2 Kings 19.

It is conjectured that the mechanism that God and the angel used for this destruction was a great bolide (meteor that explodes just above the earth's surface or impacts it) that exploded just above the Assyrian camp. This is at the time of the last close "flyby" of Mars, which comes so close that its orbit becomes permanently changed along with Earth's. Mars will pass just in front of Earth a mere 70,000 miles away. Mars first appears in the morning sky about 8:00 AM and will be about 50 times larger than the moon in size and that evening will shine 75 times brighter than a full moon. In Mars' wake is a large train of meteors, many of which will enter Earths atmosphere. One of  the larger ones arrives directly over the Assyrian camp and explodes in the atmosphere just before impact. To say that the Assyrians are destroyed is an understatement. 185,000 die although Sennacherib the blasphemous Assyrian King survives but is badly burned. [158] Other devastating affects are felt around the world and several biblical record those around Jerusalem.

Eyewitness Descriptions of the Isaiah Catastrophe

Consider Psalm 46 which is thought by some to be composed by Isaiah, who was a witness to the final "close fly by" in 701 BC.

---

[158] As stated by Ginzberg in his work: "Legends of the Jews – Vol VI pp 362-363" although it is proposed there that the burning should not be taken literally, it is suggested by Patten that it should be literal - as quoted in "The Long Day of Joshua"; page 38

V	Passage	Affects in the Earth
1	God is our refuge and strength, A very present help in rouble,	
2	Therefore we will not fear, thought the earth should change [be removed] and though the mountains slip into the heart of the sea	Orbital shift Crustal deformation
3	Though its waters roar and foam, though the mountains quake at its swelling pride	Giant tidal waves Crustal deformation and Earthquakes
5	God is in the midst of her, she will not be moved....	
6	The nations made an uproar, the kingdome tottered He raised His voice, the earth melted	Assyrians Vulcanism
8	Come, behold the works of the Lord, Who has wroght desolations in the earth.	180,000 died in the night
9	He makes wars to cease to the end of the earth; He breaks the bow and cuts the spear in tow; He burns the chariots with fire	Assyrian war Bolides (Meteors)
10	Cease striving and know that I am God I will be exalted among the nations, I will be exalted in the earth	Spiritual Awareness
11	The Lord of hosts is with us; The God of Jacob is our stronghold	God will triumph

Shocking statements found in Psalm 46

Micah the prophet was a contemporary of Isaiah and made the following prediction concerning the coming judgment:
*"For behold, the Lord is coming forth from His place. He will come down and tread on the high places of the earth. The **mountains will melt** under Him and the **valleys will be split, like wax before the fire**, like water poured down a steep place"* Micah 1:3-4

Habakkuk was a youth at the time of the Isaiah event and later recorded these words:
*"His radiance is like the sunlight; He has rays flashing from His hand, And there is the hiding of His power. Before Him goes **pestilence**, and **plague [bruning coals – KJV]** comes after Him. He stood and **surveyed the earth**; He looked and startled the nations. Yes, the perpetual **mountains were shattered**, the **ancient hills collapsed**. His ways are everlasting. I saw the tents of Cushan under distress, the tent curtains of the land of Midian were trembling. Did the Lord **rage against the rivers**, or was you anger against the rivers, or was your wrath against the sea……you **cleaved the earth with rivers**. The **mountains saw you and quaked**; the downpour of waters swept by. The **deep uttered forth its voice**, it lifted high its hands. **Sun and moon stood in their places**; At the radiance of Your gleaming spear. In indignation You marched through the earth; in anger Your trampled the nations. Your went forth for the salvation of Your people, For the salvation of your anointed."* Habakkuk 3:4-13

- Pestilence: (Hebrew *deber*) is also used in the Exodus catastrophe and *deber* is variously translated as "plague" and "murrain" and 18 different words. May represent bolides, since it is used to describe falling fragments catastrophe after catastrophe

- Burning coals: (Hebrew *resheph*) suggesting a burning arrow flashing through the air, burning heat, a hot thunderbolt, a spark....is the equivalent to meteors
- Surveyed: (Hebrew *muwd*) sometimes translated "to measure" but from the root word meaning "to shake."
- Quaked: (Hebrew *chiyl*) suggest to twist, to writhe, to dance, to travail

Isaiah initially was bringing God's message of coming destruction to all he earth: "*From the Lord of hosts you will be punished with thunder and earthquake and loud noise, with whirlwind and tempest and the flame of a consuming fire.*" (Isaiah 29:6) But after Hezekiah turns to the Lord and calls upon the city to do also, God spares them from the destruction, however not the Assyrians. Isaiah then brings the news from God that He will strike the Assyrians: ""*Thus says the Lord, "Do not be afraid because of the words that thou hast heard, wherewith the servants of the King of Assyria have blasphemed me. Behold, I will send a blast upon him, and he shall hear a rumor, and return to his own land; and I will cause him to fall by the sword in his own land.*" (Isaiah 37:6-7 – KJV) It is proposed by Patten that a bolide exploded above the Assyrian camp outside Jerusalem causing the death of the 185,000.

Consider:
- Job 38:22-23 "*Have you entered the storehouses of the snow, or have you seen the storehouses of the hail, Which I have reserved for the time of distress, for the day of war and battle?*" (NAS)
- Psalm 148:8 "*Fire and hail, snow and clouds; Stormy wind, fulfilling His word;*" (NAS)

Why do We Care? What about the Future?

The key to understanding the future is to understand the past. God always acts in a consistent, deliberate and REVEALED manner. God has stated He does nothing without "revealing" it first. Why? Because that validates He is God, able to bring His purposes to pass. So, to understand what is going to happen, you need to study the past, to understand God's methods as described in the Holy Scriptures, and then relate it to God revealed plan that is contained in His prophecy. Consider the following:

5 – Astronomy and Cosmology

Ever wonder why hundreds of thousands of citizens of Nineveh, after centuries of following false gods and various idols suddenly turned, repented and became believers and followers of the True and living God, the God of Israel? It is perhaps the greatest miracle of the entire Old Testament. Think of it, some 600,000 [159] people turning in unison to a saving faith in the Creator God. A revival so great, so quick, so massive, that it has never been in all of history. In just days, 10's of thousands turn from bowing to idols, to destroying them and falling before the God of Mercy, begging forgiveness and pleading for mercy. Yes, there was this man, a very reluctant preacher, who had just marched through the city proclaiming that it was about to be destroyed by the True God, the God of Israel. If one did that today, he would be quickly laughed off and dismissed as a wacko (that is a technical term for someone who's elevator doesn't go all the way to the top). So, why would all these people abandon their religious beliefs, for something different? Consider the following.

One of the gods of the Assyrians was Dagon - a fish type creature

It has been a while, but the planet Mars is due for a close flyby in just a few weeks. Stories of ancient catastrophes are circulated once again as anxious citizens consider possible scenarios. Perhaps this one will destroy them. Perhaps this one will destroy their enemies. Then on September 15, 754 BC (the exact date isn't known), a man claiming to be a prophet enters the city with this fantastic story of how he ran from God, survived being eaten by a 'Large Fish" and now, was there to declare God's coming judgment. Nineveh was to fall in 40 days, will all its citizens with it. They had been following the wrong god's, the gods of stone and wood. The Creator God was calling for justice. In a very surprising move, the King of the nation, knowing of the approaching planet that has brought destruction, mayhem and doom to the earth many times, decides to abandon his previous beliefs and turn to God and beg for mercy. In faith, he places his life in the hands of the Living God, a smart move in general, and subsequently, the entire city follows.

---

[159] "The Bible Exposition Commentary – Old Testament – The Prophets"; Warren Wiersbe; Victor – Cook Communications; copyright 2002; page 383

Meanwhile, across town, Uzziah, King of Israel who has had a good lengthy reign, is getting nervous. Uzziah was a good king, he had been following God from his youth, becoming king at the age of 16 and now, after more than 40 years of service he was very wealthy, and very powerful. Because he had faithfully followed God, God had blessed him. He had amassed great wealth. This led to a weakness that often accompanies success, pride. Uzziah was becoming a prideful person and it was beginning to drive his behavior. As the planet of Mars began to draw closer, Uzziah decided that he should be the one to enter the Temple of God at Jerusalem and offer the offerings and sacrifices. Forbidden by God to do so, Uzziah begins to move in that direction. God had established the Levis as priests, the only ones allowed to perform the temple service. Kings were of the line of Judah, and descendants of King David through Solomon and only they could sit on the throne. Uzziah was a king (decendent of Solomon) and therefore by definition he was not a priest nor perform priestly duties (Jesus is the only one who will hold the office of prophet, priest and king).

It is October 25, 756 BC and around 2:00 pm Mars rises in the eastern sky of Jerusalem. It is ¾ solar lit and will diminish to a slit by the end of the evening. It will come within a mere 100,000 miles (the moon is 239,000 miles from earth) of the earth and will be about 20 times the size of a full moon in the sky. I'm sure some witty Israelite quipped upon seeing the awesome sight: "this can't be good!" The city of Nineveh is in prayer, pleading with God, the living God, for their salvation. Back in Jerusalem, Uzziah enters the Temple of the

5 – Astronomy and Cosmology

Living God and against great protests of the priests, begins to prepare to offer sacrifices, an unwise move on his part and one that he will live to regret. Disaster ensues. Nineveh, in humble prayer is spared, much to the chagrin of Jonah, who detested the ruthless Assyrians (Ninevites). Uzziah, acting in pride is about to become humbled. Uzziah enters the temple proper and God's wrath begins to pour out. With the two planets in close proximity, land masses begin to pull at each other and mighty earthquakes ensue. Jerusalem is rocked to the core an a large landmass of the mountains around Jerusalem literally breaks off and a landslide ensues. Shaken into a flowing mass, a wave of rocks and earth crashes into the city as people scatter for their lives, mayhem breaks out. Solomon's Temple, which is one of the seven wonders of the ancient world and now over 500 years old, cracks open at the roof and a ray of sunlight pours

in striking Uzziah. Leprosy, the dreaded disease of the ancient and modern world breaks out on his face. The priests gape and Uzziah flees the scene, and is forced to live alone and isolated with his affliction the remainder of his life living.

By now, the skeptics are jumping out of the wood work questioning the veracity of this little episode that has just been unfolded. What are the facts as we know them?

- Fact – Jonah – prophet of God; called of God; lived 3 days in a fish; preached at Nineveh; saw the entire city repent and be spared - see Jonah 1 also attested to by Jesus (Matt 12:39-41 and Luke 11:29-39)
- Fact – Uzziah – Good King who in pride entered the temple to make sacrifices to God violating Deuteronomy and was struck with leprosy as a result (2 Chron 26)
- History – The great earthquake and the ensuing landslide are recorded by Josephus, the famed historian living during the time of Christ. He writes: "While Uzziah...was corrupted in his mind by pride....on account of that abundance which he had of things that will soon perished...carried headlong into the sins of his fathers... went into the temple to offer incense...which he was prohibited to do....In the meantime, a great earthquake shook the ground, and a rent was made in the temple, and the bright rays of the sun shone through it, and fell upon the king's face, insomuch that the leprosy seized upon him

immediately; and before the city, at a place called Eroge, half the mountain broke off from the rest on the west, and rolled itself four furlongs, and stood still at the east mountain, till the roads, as well as the king's gardens, were spoiled by the obstruction" [160]

- Conjecture – Close flyby of Mars as the cause of the physical catastrophe – Proposed by Patten et all [161]
- Conjecture supported – But wait, there's more.

Now, lets put some history and prophecy together for an amazing result. In case this all seems a little, or a lot, outrageous, lets look back into the Bible for some facts and see what the future holds. First some comments from Amos, a prophet of the time of all this:

- Amos 1:1 "what he saw two years before the earthquake, when Uzziah was king....The Lord roars from Zion and thunders from Jerusalem; the pastures of the shepherds dry up"
- Amos 2:5 "I will send fire upon Judah that will consume the fortresses of Jerusalem"

Some 200 years after this event, God raises up the prophet Zechariah. Zechariah is given some staggering prophecies which span all the way from ancient Israel up through the time of the Millennium. One of these fascinating prophecies concerns the return of the Lord, His second coming. Zechariah speaks of the Lords Return; *"and the Mount of Olives will be split in two from east to west, forming a great valley, with half of the mountain moving north and half moving south....**you will flee as you fled from the earthquake in the days of Uzziah king of the Judah**...Then the Lord my God will come, and all the holy ones with him* [that's us!]" (NIV). Wow, history illuminating prophecy. Oh, and by the way, don't miss the part where we come in. Jesus, when He returns to earth to set up His Millennial Kingdom, we will be coming with Him. We, the Bride of Christ will be part of the "Host of Heaven."

---

[160] "The Antiquities of the Jews" - Book IX - Chapter 10: 4: 222-225 –Josephus; see "The Works of Josephus" Translated by William Whiston; Hendrickson Pub; copyright 1987; page 260-261

[161] "Long Day of Joshua"; Patten; page 99 and 151

Other biblical accounts of future cosmic catastrophes include the following:

Although there are two different sequences of events in Revelation prophesied to occur during the tribulation, there are similarities. The first sequence (Seal Judgments – Rev 6) will effect ¼ of the earth and the second sequence (Trumpet – Rev 8) effects 1/3 of the earth. A final series (Bowl or Vial Judgments) occurs at the end, the return of Christ to earth (Rev 16)

	Matt 24:3-29	Joel 2:2-31	Isa 13:6-13	Rev 6:12-17	Rev 8:5-12	Rev 16:18
Sun	Darkened	Dark	Dark	Turns black	1/3 Darkned	
Moon	Not give its light	Dark - blood	Dark	Turns red - like blood	1/3 Darkned	
Stars	Fall from the sky	Loose brightness	Dim	Stars fall - like ripe figs	1/3 Darkned	
Heavens	Powers of heaven will be shaken	Tremble	Tremble	Sky split and rolls up		
Earth-quake		Earth quakes	Earth shakes	Great earthquake Mountains and Islands moved		Greatest ever on the earth
Other					Thunder, lighting, great burning mountain thrown	Islands and mountains flee, huge hailstones

Table of End Times Cosmic Events [162]

Jesus on the end time (Tribulation): Matthew 24:3, 7, 29 (also see Mark 13:24-25) *"...Tell us, when will these things happen, and what will be the sign of Your coming, and the end of the age?....for nation will rise against nation, and kingdom against kingdom, and in various places there will be famines and **earthquakes**....but immediately after the tribulation of those days **the sun will be darkened, and the moon will not give its lights, and the stars will fall from the sky, and the powers of the heavens will be shaken**...*"

The prophet Joel on the Tribulation: Joel 2:2, 10, 30-31 *"A day of darkness and gloom, A day of clouds and thick darkness...Before them **the earth quakes, the heavens tremble, the sun and the moon grow dark, and the stars lose their brightness... I will display wonders in the sky and on the earth, blood, fire and columns of smoke. The sun will be turned into darkness and the moon into blood** before the great and awesome day of the Lord comes."*

---

[162] Table concept from: "Astronomy and the Bible"; Donald DeYoung; Baker Book House; copyright 1989; 11th printing 1994; page 113

The prophet Isaiah on the tribulation: Isaiah 13:6, 10, 13 *"Wail, for the day of the Lord is near!... For the stars of heaven and their constellations will not flash forth their light; the sun will be dark when it rises and the moon will not shed its lights...therefore **I will make the heavens tremble**, and the **earth will be shaken from its place.**"*

Isaiah 24:1, 6, 18b-21 *"Behold, **the Lord lays the earth waste, devastates it, distorts its surface and scatters its inhabitants**...Therefore, a curse devours the earth, and those who live in it are held guilty. Therefore, the **inhabitants of the earth are burned**, and few men are left...for the **windows above are opened, and the foundations of the earth shake. The earth is broken asunder, the earth is split through, the earth is shaken violently. The earth reels to and fro like a drunkard and it totters like a shack,** for its transgression is heavy upon it, and it will fall, never to rise again. So it will happen in that day, that the Lord will punish the host of heaven on high, and the kings of the earth on earth."*

John in Revelation describes several instances of cosmic disruption during the Tribulation: Revelation 6:12-17 *"I looked when He broke the sixth seal, and there was a **great earthquake**; and the **sun became black as sackcloth made of hair, and the whole moon became like blood; and the stars of the sky fell to the earth**, as a fig tree casts its unripe figs when shaken by a great wind. The **sky was split apart** like a scroll when it is rolled up, and **every mountain and island were moved out of their places**. The kings of the earth and the great men and the commanders and the rich and the strong and every slave and free man hid themselves in the caves and among the rocks of the mountains; and they said to the mountains and to the rocks, "Fall on us and hide us from the presence of Him who sits on the throne, and from the wrath of the Lamb; for the great day of their wrath has come, and who is able to stand?""*

Revelation 8:5, 7, 8, 10, 12
*"...and there followed **peals of thunder and sounds and flashes of lightning and an earthquake**...and there came **hail and fire, mixed with blood, and they were thrown to the earth**; and a third of the earth was burned up....and something like a great mountain burning with fire was thrown into the sea; and a third of the sea became blood....and a **great star fell from heaven, burning like a torch,** and it fell on the a third of the rivers and on the springs of waters...and a third of the sun and a third of the moon and a third of the stars were struck, so that a third of them would be darkened and the day would not shine for a third of it, and the night in the same way..."*

5 – Astronomy and Cosmology

Revelation 11:19 *"And the temple of God which is in heaven was opened; and the ark of His covenant appeared in His temple, and there were flashes of lightning and sounds and peals of thunder and an* **earthquake and a great hailstorm.**"

Revelation 16:18 *"And there were flashes of lightning and sounds and peals of thunder; and there was a* **great earthquake, such as there had not been since man came to be upon the earth, so great an earthquake was it, and so mighty.** *The great city was split into three parts, and the cities of the nations fell. Babylon the great was remembered before God, to give her the cup of the wine of His fierce wrath.* **And every island fled away, and the mountains were not found. And huge hailstones, about one hundred pounds each, came down from heaven** *upon men; and men blasphemed God because of the plague of the hail, because its plague was extremely severe."*

Zechariah describing the return of Christ to the earth: Zech 14: 4-8
"In that day His [Messiah's] feet will stand on the Mount of Olives, which is in front of Jerusalem on the east; and the Mount of Olives will be split in its middle from east to west by a very large valley, so that half of the mountain will move toward the north and the other half toward the south. Your will flee by the valley of My mountains, for the valley of the mountains will reach to Azel; yes, you will flee just as you fled before the earthquake in the days of Uzziah king of Judah. Then the Lord, my God, will come, and all the holy ones with Him! IN that day there will be no light; the luminaries will dwindle. For it will be a unique day which is known to the Lord, neither day nor night, but it will come about that at evening time there will be light. And in that day living waters will flow out of Jerusalem, half of them toward the eastern sea and the other half toward the western sea; it will be in summer as well as in winter."

Asteroid Trivia:

- Earth accumulates about 100 tons of extraterrestrial material every day
- An asteroid about 50 meters packs about 10 megatons of energy
- 1972 Narrow miss by a similar size meteor
- Oct 1992 media broke the news that a comet strike was likely but then changed to 8 more orbits
- Comet "Swift-Tuttle" passes every 130 years, each time a little closer
- Jan 23, 1982 an asteroid 1/3 of a mile in diameter passes 2.5 million miles from earth without being observed until a month later
- March 22, 1989, a closer near miss (by 6 hours (400,000 miles))
- Tunguska (central Siberia) was hit June 30, 1908 devastating over 2,000 square miles
- Winslow, AZ creater similar to the Tuguska strike
- Experts estimate that 15 megaton energy hits occur once every 300 years on the Earth's surface, about once every millenium on land
- 1991 discovery of crater (Chicxulub) in the Yucatan peninsula is conjectured to have resulted in the extinction of the dinosaurs (6 miles in diameter carrying 100 million megatons)

5 – Astronomy and Cosmology

Chapter 5.7

Gospel in the Stars

Job 38:32
"Canst thou bring forth Mazzaroth in his season? or canst thou guide Arcturus with his sons? ..." (KJV)

"Can you lead forth a constellation in its season, And guide the Bear with her satellites?" (NAS)

Purpose of the Zodiac

We need to quickly dismiss the false notion that the stars and constellations known as the Zodiac are somehow prophetic of individuals and based on your birth date, you can fortune tell your future and gain advise. This is a pagan concept and directly opposes many scriptural aspects of the Bible. So, this is NOT what we are looking at in this chapter. What we ARE looking at is the potential that God ordained a method of describing His overall plan for man from the beginning of the universe by arranging the stars of the universe in certain patterns which upon study, reveal stories and insight into Gods magnificent plan. God's plan for  redemption of the universe was established prior to the formation of the universe itself. God has not been adjusting His plan to fit a set of changing circumstances. God is bringing His sovereign will to pass while allowing man the freedom to chose to be obedient to Him or be disobedient and advancing the cause of evil. God has allowed evil to reign for a season but will ultimately bring it into destruction. We can see an example of this in Genesis 3 where, after the fall of man, God states that a redeemer is coming and that "His head shall bruise his heel" referring to the fact that even though the redeemer ("seed of the woman" – even indicates a virgin birth) will eventually conqueror the "seed of the serpent" a "bruising" would occur. We see this played out as Christ paid the penalty for our sins and died in our place. The good news, however, was that He was resurrected and now reigns in the Heavens and soon on the earth.

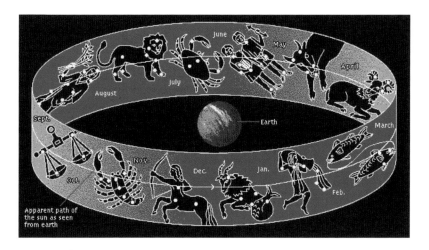

Realizing that God's plan was developed and has been communicated via scriptures and includes the prophetic element which incidentally establishes the fact that He is the Almighty God, the question before us is, was any of this communicated prior to the recording of the scriptures by Moses around 1500 BC. What about that first 2,500 years? Did anyone understand God's plan of a savior and redemption?

A provocative conjecture has been advanced stating that the original zodiac, is not what we have today (although there are very strong links) but the meaning of the signs of the Heavens were different in the beginning. Of importance to note is that Josephus, writing at the time of Christ, states that this was indeed the case and that the Hebrews knew the signs and their meanings. They were apparently developed by Seth, Adam's direct descendent. Josephus speaking of Seth and his children: "They were also inventors of that peculiar sort of wisdom which is concerned with the heavenly bodies and their order." [163] It is generally believed that this original understanding was corrupted during the Babylonian times of the Tower of Babel as was many other heinous idolatries established at that time. Because of this origin, large similarities exist between zodiacs today and the original.

---

[163] "The Works of Josephus"; translated by William Whiston; Hendrickson pub.; copyright 1983; 16th printing , Aug 2001; "Antiquities of the Jews; Book 1, Chapter 2, Section 3"; Page 32

Diligent study was made in this area near the end of the 1800's and two great works were published on the subject. Both are available in reprint today. E.W. Bulllinger wrote on and begins his study with the following comment: "For more than two thousand five hundred years the world was without a written revelation from God. The question is; Did God leave Himself without a witness?" [164] The second work is by Joseph Seiss who after delineating a strong case of evidences for this concept makes the following statement; "that the only true answer to the origin is the one given in the text [Bible], which unequivocally ascribes it to the inspiration of God, who by His Spirit garnished the heavens and with His own hand bent the traditional ring of their goings." [165]

Popular scholars who have given credit to this thought include; Henery M. Morris [166] ; D. James Kennedy who wrote a book on the subject [167] and Chuck Missler [168].

Biblical Support of Mazzaroth:

In God's discourse to Job, establishing the fact that God is God and man is only man, makes reference to the "Mazzaroth" the Jewish Zodiac and one of its signs. Job, being the oldest writing of the scriptures, indicates the ancient age of the Mazzaroth making the implication that the signs are from God. See Job 38:32 Additionally, earlier in Job there appears a specific reference to the creation of the signs by God in Job 26:13; *"By his spirit he hath garnished the heavens; his hand hath formed the crooked serpent"* (KJV) The serpent is a reference to either Draco or Hydra, the serpent.

Additionally, in Psalm 19: 1-4, we find what appears to be a reference to meaning behind the Zodiac. *"The heavens declare the glory of God; the skies*

---

[164] "The Witness of the Stars"; E.W.Bullinger; Kregel Pub; first published 1893; reprint 2000; Page 1
[165] "The Gospel in the Stars"; Joseph Seiss; Kregel Pub; originally published 1882; reprint 1972; page 23
[166] "The Long War Against God" Henry Morris; Baker Book House Company; copyright 1989; 5th printing 11/1992; pages 265-267
[167] "The Real Meaning of the Zodiac"; D. James Kennedy; TCRM Pub; June 1989
[168] "Cosmic Codes"; Chuck Missler; Koinonia House; Copyright 1999; page 200-201

proclaim the work of his hands. Day after day they pour forth speech; night after night they display knowledge. There is no speech or language where their voice is not heard. Their voice goes out into all the earth, their words to the ends of the world." It is certainly true that just the basic thought of the creation comes from seeing stars in the sky but something more seems to be here.

Indeed, it would seem that this was intended from the very beginning. Consider Genesis 1:14, the creation of the "lights" in the sky, the stars; "*Then God said, "Let there be lights in the expanse of the heavens to separate the day from the night, and let them be for signs and for seasons and for days and years.*" The constellations are not just to mark seasons, it clearly states separately they are for **SIGNS**. Seiss: "And thus when God said of the celestial luminaries, "and let them be for signs," He meant that they should be used to signify something beyond and additional to what they evidence and express in their nature and natural offices." [169]

Ascertaining the Meaning of a Constellation:

The Mazzaroth consists of 12 constellations. Each month, a new constellation takes it turn in starting on the eastern horizon of the night sky and every night they rotate thought the night sky as the sun does in the day. Consistency exists between the ancient 30-day month and 12-month year forming the 360-day year (see chapter 5.6 for background) as the 12 zodiacal signs. Each sign consists of a major constellation and three minor constellations referred to as Decans. Each of the three decans provides additional understanding and compliments the major sign. Of further insight are the names of the stars in the constellation. These stars can provide further clarity in the understanding of the story.
Sphinx

Because the constellations follow each other every month, there is a question as to where to start the story. Bullinger points out that the Egyptians have left us a great monument to solve this problem. Their zodiac, similar to others, had it's beginning with Virgo (the virgin mother – sounds like a good place to start) and ends with Leo (the Lion). This is depicted in by the Great Sphinx (word means "to bind closely together") which has the head of a woman and the body of a lion. Bullinger; "Virgo is the only point where we can intelligently begin, and Leo is the only point where we can logically conclude. Is not this what is spoken of as the unknown and insoluble mystery – "the riddle of the

---

[169] "The Gospel in the Stars"; J.A. Seiss; page 11

Sphinx"?...It was there fore designed to show where the two ends of the Zodiac were to be jointed together.." [170]

I'll propose that the overall story can be broken into three main sections, with 4 constellations each. The first group depicts a dual natured (God-Man) redeemer, born of a virgin who will pay the price required and conquer the enemy serpent. The second group depicts the sacrifice made and the church, which rises from the living waters of the deliverer and the ruling "Ram". The final group indicates what is still to come giving us the picture of wrath and judgement being brought upon the earth and establishment of the earthly reign of the Redeemer ruling with His bride, the church. Look into the following and see if you conclude the same.

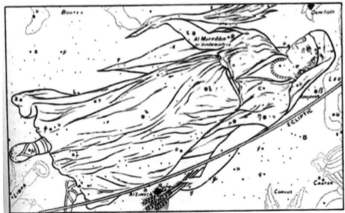

---

[170] ""The Witness of the Stars"; Bullinger; page 20

First 4 Constellations – 1st Group:

The person, the work and triumph are depicted in the first set of constellations of the Mazzaroth. A word picture summary of what was already taken place.

Virgo - Virgin (speaks of the virgin birth of Christ - the beginning of earthy time)		
Al Zimach - the Shoot	Al Azal - the Branch (Jesus is the	Subilon - Ear of Wheat
Coma - the Infant, the Branch, the Desired One - woman admiring an infant child (Jesus from Haggai; "the desire of all nations")	Centaurus - Centaur with dart piercing a victim - centaur has two natures (Jesus has a double nature; God and Man)	Bootes or Archturus - great Shepherd and Harvester (with rod and sickle) (Jesus said; "I am the good Shepherd") Bootes also means "the coming one"
Libra - the Scales		
Zeben al Genubi - the Price deficient	Zuben al Shemali - the Price which	Al Gubi - Heaped up High
Crux - the Cross (where Jesus paid the price)	Lupus or Victima - the Wolf or Victim (Jesus was the slain one) (the victum is slain by the Centar or Virgo - it is Jesus who offers Himself)	Corona - the Crown - (Jesus will wear the crown of the King of Kings)
Scorpio, the scorpion - also means wounding, conflict, war		
Antares - wounding, cutting or		
Serpens, the Serpent - Evil Spirit, the Dragon, that old serpent, the Devil and Satan)	Ophiuchus, the serpent holder (Jesus restrains the serpent who is reaching for the crown) (the man Ophiucus has his foot on Scorpio's head)	Hercules - man holding a club striking serpents in his other hand - (Jesus came to bruise the serpent, the devil) (also referred to as "the branch kneeling and the head of him who bruises)
Sagittarius, the Archer - Centaur with bow and arrow (picture of the royal Messiah - the arrow is aimed at the heart of the Scorpion)		
Vega - brightest star in the North - meaning "He shall be exalted, He shall triumph" - it is the root for the English = Victory		
Lyra, the Harp (Eagle shaped - in some depictions) (Instrument of Praise seen in the picture of Heaven in Revelation 5 and XX)	Ara, the Altar or burning pyre or funeral pyre Hebrew *mara* and *aram;* connates a curse brought to ruin	Draco, the Dragon (or serpent) cast down Key stars; Al Waid, who is to be destroyed; Thuban, the subtle; Al Dib, the reptile

- Virgo – the Virgin; picture of the virgin Mary who brings forth the infant child, the "shoot of the branch" the dual natured God-Man who is our shepherd
- Libra – the Scales; picture of sin weighed in the balance, the price thereby deficient but, good news, there is a cross, a sacrifice and a crown for the one who triumphs. Jesus the Christ is the Lamb that was slain, on the cross and will reign as our King.

- Scorpio – the scorpion in conflict and war, contains *Serpens* the serpent, the dragon, the devil who is reaching for the crown but is restrained and is struck (bruised) by the man Hercules.
- Sagittarius - the Dual Natured Bowman, the triumphal archer with arrow aimed at scorpion, depicts Christ's God-Human duality and is accompanied by the harp of praise, the funeral pyre altar of the curse brought to an end and Draco, the serpent who is to be cast down.

I have included a table for each of the constellation groups which indicates the major constellations, in some cases key stars and for all, the three deacons.

2nd Constellation Group:

Portrayed in the next four constellations is the Redeemers future work, His mediatorship and the formation of the Church, the body of Christ and the Bride of Christ. We see "what is" depicted in these pictures, what is happening today.

Capricornus, the Goat with a fish tail (the Goat is fallen, picture of a sacrificed animal - the fish tail represents the fish (church) brought forth from the death of the Goat)		
Sagitta, the shot and killing arrow (He was pierced for our iniquity)	Aquila, the pierced wounded and falling eagle (picture of the pierced Messiah)	Delphinus, the Dolphin (picture of the church coming forward)

Aquarius, the water-bearer (man pouring water from an urn) (picture of the Lord pouring out the living waters for all to partake)		
Sa'ad al Melik (principle star) meaning Record of the outpouring		
PiscisAustralis; fish drinking in the stream from the outpouring (picture of the church, the people drinking the living waters)	Pegasus, the winged horse of the gushing fountain; formed from *Pega* meaning the chief and *sus* meaning a swiftly coming or returning horse (picture of church, ambassadors of Christ swiftly brining the good news)	Swan; lordly bird king of the waters; stars: Deneb (the lord or Jude to come)Azel (who goes and returns) Fafage (glorious, shining forth) Sadr (who returns as in a circle); Adige (flying swiftly) Arided (He shall come down) (picture of the swan, the church circling the earth preaching the news of the Great Lord and Judge who will return)

Pisces; two fish (signifying a multitude) tied to cords held by the Ram (of the next constellation) (picture of the church, the multitude coming from the waters)		
The Band or Ribbon (picture of unifying connection with the ram - the victorious lamb)	Ceheus, The Crowned King; friend and protector of the fishes; key stars; *Al Deramin* (the Quickly-returning); *Al Phirk* (the Redeemer) and (The Shepherd)	Andromeda, the chained woman; literally man-ruler; mstic woman called and appointed to rule and guardianship over men (picture of the church, the bride of Christ who will rule for Him)

Aries;the Ram, the Chief, the Head; meaning the Lordly (picture of Christ, the head of His Church)		
El Nath (the wounded)	*El Natik* (the bruised)	*Al Sharetan* (the slain)
Cassiopeia; woman seated (meaning the beautiful, the enthroned) Stars; *Shedar* (the freed) *Ruchbah* (the enthroned) *Dat al Cursa* (the seated) (picture of the church lifted up)	Cetus, the sea monster - name means The Rebel (Leviathan of Job and Isaiah) Stars; *Menkar* (the chained enemy) *Diphda* (overthrown, the thrust-down) (picture of the enemy, the one who preys upon the fishes)	Perseus, the Breaker depicted as a man with winged feet and with sword held high and carrying the snaked head of a victim; Stars; *Atik* (He who breaks) *Al Genib* (One who carries away) *Mirfak* (who helps); the head Medusa (means the trodden under foot) with stars meaning Evil Spirit and Satan's head and the weakened; (picture of triumph over Satan)

2nd Constlation Group – Capricornus – Goat with a fish tail

Capricornus – the goat fallen with a fish tail depicts Christ as our sacrifice being pierced by a killing arrow but new life, the fish, the church rises.

- Aquarius - the waterman pouring water from a large vase is Christ, pouring out the living waters to all who would receive them and alongside are fish (the church) drinking from the fountain and Pegasus, the winged horse depicting us as ambassadors for the good news and a beautiful, graceful swan foretelling of the great Ruler who is to return.

- Pisces – two fish representing the church which is connected to the victorious lamb and their protector, the crowned king, the Redeemer and Shepherd and includes Andromeda, the chained woman (the church) who will one day rule.

- Aries – the ram, the chief who is head of the church, Christ our Head, and included are Cassiopeia, the beautiful woman (church) enthroned, lifted up by Christ; a great sea monster who will be destroyed and Persus, the great warrior (Christ) with sword held high, who has victory over the enemy with its serpent head in his hand.

3rd and Last Constellation Group:

Taurus, the Bull enraged (picture of Christ bringing the coming judgment)		
Al Debaran (the Captian, Leader or Governor)		
Orion - a mighty man holding a club and the skin of a lion with foot over a rabbit enemy; (Orion means = He who cometh forth as light, the Brilliant, the Swift) stars; *Betelguese* (The Branch coming) *Rigel* (the foot that crusheth) and a 3 cluster known as the three kings and Jacob's rod (picture of Christ defeating the enemy)	Eridanus, The River (name means River of the Judge) (picture of the river of fire, of judgment)	Auriga, The Shepherd (mighty man seated holding a band or ribbon in his right hand and a she-goat in the left (she-goat is looking in astonishment upon the terrible bull) (picture of church safely in the arms of the mighty man while the bull charges)
Gemini, The Twins (picture of Christ and His church, the marriage union)		
Al Henah (the Hurt, the Wounded)	Polux (the Ruler, the Judge)	Wasat (set, seated or put in place)
Lepus; the hare or rabbit is about to be crushed by the foot of Orion; Stars; *Nibal* (the Mad), *Rakis* (the caught), *Sugia* (the deceiver) (picture of the enemy being defeated by the Lord)	Sirius, (Canis Major) the great Dog or ancient, the wolf; in the Dendera Zodiac it is depicted as an Eagle or Hawk, enemy of the serpent: Stars *Sirius* (Prince, Guardian, the Victorius); *Mirzam* (the ruler) *Muliphen* (the leader, the Chieftain) *Wesen* (Shining, illustrious, scarlet) *Adhara* (the Glorious) *Al Habor* (the Might) (picture of the Sublime Prince, the Naz-Seir-ene, the appointed prince)	Canis Minor, the companion; Egyptian zodiac it is a man's body with eagle's head; Stars; *Procyon* (implies Redeemed); *Al Mirzam* (rulership) *Al Gomeiza* (Redemption, also implying historical, onced burdened) (picture of the church, following the Ruler similar but different, come to rule)
Cancer, the Crab; Egyptians *Klaria,* meaning the folds or resting-places; specifically Can-cer means Rest Secured (picture of Church coming to take it's place)		
Acubens - the sheltering, the palce of retirement, the good rest	Praesepe (the Multitude, Offspring, the young, the innumerable seed)	Maalaph and Al Himarein meaning assembled thousands, the kids or lambs
Ursa Minor (now called the bear) but originally a fold or collection of domestic animals; sever key stars known as thoses which go around, associated with the kings chariot wheels (picture of the church - 7 churches)	Ursa Major - Ancient, the Great Sheepfold; Star *Mizar* (garded or enclosed place) *Dubheh* (herd or fold) *Merach* (the flock) *Cab d al Asad* (multitude of the assembled) (picture of the church brought into protection and blessing)	Argo, th e Ship Stars *Canopus* (the possession of Him who comes) *Sephina* (multitudinous good, the very abundance) *Tureis* (firm possession in hand) *Asmidiska* (the travellers released) *soheil* (what was desired) (picture of church at rest)
Leo, the Lion (picture of the "Lion of the Tribe of Judah" Jesus the Christ, the Messaiah)		
Hydra, the Serpent (name means abhorred) Star Al Phard (the sparated, the excluded, the put out of the way) constellation Minchir al Sugia (the punishing, or teraring to pieces, of the decilever) (picture of Satan and evil being brought to an end)	Crater, the Cup of Wrath (picture of wrath being associated with the serpent and his forces)	Corvus, the Raven; Egyptians (the enemy broken) Star, Al Chiba (the curse inflicted) constellation Minchir al Gorab (Raven teraring to pieces) (picture of ravens dining on the fallen foes)

These constellations tell us of the coming consummation of all things, when our Lord will return to earth and establish His rule with the believers at His side.

- Taurus - the Bull (picturing Christ) is a rushing animal bring wrath upon the earth has three signs, Orion, the might man, the branch who comes forth as light triumphing over His enemies, Eridanus the judgment river of fire and Auriga (Jesus) the great shepherd holding the young she-goat protectively as the Bull does His work
- Gemini – the twins showing the integral relationship between Christ and His Church including the deceiver caught, the Ruling Prince and his similar but different associate (church).
- Cancer – the Crab provides us a picture of a great multitude, collected together now brought to their true rest, brought into protection and care and like a ship come to port, bringing great abundance and finally at rest
- Leo – the lion which is Christ, the Lion of the Tribe of Judah who has come to earth to reign and includes three signs, Hydra-the serpent being destroyed; Crater-the cup of wrath being poured out and Corvus-the raven dinning on the destroyed serpent.

Constellation – Leo – The Lion

5 – Astronomy and Cosmology

Chapter 6.1

Hyperspace Buildings – 4+ Dimensions

Hebrews 8:4-5: *"Now if He [Jesus] were on earth, He would not be a priest at all, since there are those who offer the gifts according to the Law; who **serve a copy and shadow of the heavenly things**, just as Moses was warned by God when he was about to erect the tabernacle; for "See," he says, "that you make all thing according to the pattern which was shown you on the mountain."* (NAS) (emphasis mine)

Copy (Greek - *hupodeigma*); definition – "figure", "copy", "example" [171]
Shadow (Greek – *skia*); definition – "shadow" [172] [173]

Section 6 is a very challenging section, both spiritually as well as in physics. I am introducing the concept that the universe that we know, really has more than just 3 dimensions plus time. We usually think of moving being limited to up, down and sideways or 3 dimensions and we also move through time, a 4th dimension. Buckle you seat belts because the scriptures indicate that there are more dimensions to this universe. There is at least one additional dimension for the spiritual world or spiritual realm. Modern physics has shattered our understanding of the physical world and now (in just the last 20 years) have proven that there are some 10 dimensions to the space-time continuum that we know. This really challenges what we think we understand but being that modern physics seems to have proven might just be what the scriptures have been telling us all along.

The fact that there is a real temple in Heaven, served in by Jesus who is the real High Priest is shocking in itself. Additionally, to understand that the Heavenly temple [Rev 16:17 - NKJ], is an actual 4 dimensional structure blows the socks off our feet. We build and live in 3 dimensional structures, some of which are very complex. All but mathematicians and small children can not even envision a 4 dimensional structure. God has communicated this knowledge to

---

[171] Strongs #5262 – page 1574
[172] Strongs #4639 – page 1565
[173] Also, *"skia"* is further defined as "shadow thrown by an object"; "New International Dictionary of New Testament Theology – Vol 3"; Collin Brown general editor; Zondervan; copyright 1967, 1986; page 554

us using a 2 dimensional (2D) to 3 dimensional (3D) analogy which helps us understand a 3D to 4D truth.

In reference to the heavenly tabernacle structure (Heb 8:4-5), God refers to it as a "shadow" of the real thing. I love riding home from work in the afternoon on my motorcycle. I can look down and see my shadow following me on the ground. My shadow looks great. It looks just like me on my bike however; it is only a silhouette, a 2d object. Not that it isn't a real thing, it is. I can see it and watch it move and change, however it is far short of my "real" 3D motorcycle (interestingly I ride a Honda Shadow). The shadow (silhouette) is 2D, my motorcycle enjoys an additional dimension and is 3D. The heavenly Temple is constructed in 4D, and God refers to this and illustrates the point by referring to our 3D structure here on earth as a mere "shadow."

One day, after we are resurrected in our 4D (or more) bodies, we will visit the 4D temple in Heaven. That will be a fascinating day! Kenneth Wuest commented; "it [the shadow] merely is proof of the fact that there is a reality back of it. It is not itself solid or real. Just so, the earthly tabernacle is proof of the fact that there was a real one, the heavenly one where God Himself dwelt, where Messiah officiates as High Priest. The Aaronic priests performed their priestly rites in representation of the heavenly tabernacle." [174]

Other References:
Hyperspace food????
Colossians 2:16-17; "*Therefore let no one act as your judge in regard to food or drink or in respect to a festival or a new moon or a Sabbath day – **things which are a mere shadow of what is to come**; but the substance belongs to Christ.*" (NAS) (emphasis mine).

Shadow (Greek – *skia*) – shadow (see previous)
Substance (Greek – *soma*); literally "body" [175]

Some of this I can comprehend. God established festivals (holidays) such as the Passover, as a representation (shadow) of the real thing to come. As an example, the Passover was a real historic festival event in which a lamb without spot or blemish was sacrificed and it's blood was painted over the doors of the families as a covering or protection from the death angle who passed through Egypt. Totally, a real historic event. However, God

---

[174] "Wuest's Word Studies from the Greek New Testament – Vol 2"; Kenneth Wuest; Eerdmans; copyright 1947, 1973 – reprint 2002
[175] "New International Dictionary of New Testament Theology"; page 556

established it to point towards a more real, important event of Jesus being offered as a lamb without spot (1 Peter 1:9) on the cross and His blood was shed for our sins (Hebrews 9:14) so we cold have eternal life.

How food and drink are only a "shadow" representing the "substance" of what is to come is a mystery to me. Perhaps there is something here in reference to the "Tree of Life" in Revelation 22 that we will eat from in the New Heaven and New Jerusalem? Interesting!

Hyperspace Jerusalem:
Hebrews 12:22-24; *"But ye are come unto mount Zion, and unto the city of the living God, **the heavenly Jerusalem**, and to an innumerable company of angels, To the general assembly and church of the firstborn, which are written in heaven, and to God the Judge of all, and to the spirits of just men made perfect, And to Jesus the mediator of the new covenant, and to the blood of sprinkling, that speaketh better things than that of Abel."* (emphasis author)

Without question, there is a heavenly, or hyperspace city of Jerusalem currently in use and underway. In fact, we learn from verse 24 that Jesus is there which confirms the fact that He "sat down at the right hand of the Father."

It is astonishing to realize that Abraham understood this an was looking forward to this city: *"By faith Abraham, when he was called, obeyed by going out to a place which he was to receive for an inheritance; and he went out, not knowing where he was going. By faith he lived as an alien in the land of promise, as in a foreign land, dwelling in tents with Isaac and Jacob, fellow heirs of the same promise; **for he was looking for the city which has foundations, whose architect and builder is God**."* Hebrews 11:8-11 (emphasis author)

6 - Hyperspace

Chapter 6.2

Origin of Hyperspace Understanding

Hebrews 1:11-12
*"You, LORD, in the beginning laid the foundation of the earth and the heavens are the works of Your hands; they will perish but You remain; and they all will become old like a garment, and like a mantle **You will roll them up**; like a garment they will also be changed but You are the same, and Your ears will not come to an end."* (NAS) (emphasis author)

Genesis 1
"And God said....(spoken 10 times in the creation account)

Multiple Dimensions – Hyperspace:

The shocking fact that our 3D universe can be "rolled up" reveals some interesting insights. First, there must be an additional dimension into which the universe can be "rolled." If you roll up a piece of paper (which is 2 dimensional (2D) when flat) it becomes a 3D object. If you roll a 3D object what does it become? At least a 4D object. A second insight, the 3D universe must be "thin" in the 4th dimension,

allowing it to be "rolled." A piece of paper is really three dimensional although rather thin in one dimension and this allows it to be rolled up. A box, is also 3D however, it is thick in all dimensions and can't really be rolled up. Our universe, the space-time continuum, is apparently 4D and is thin in one direction allowing it to be rolled up.

Man has understood the 3D universe from the beginning moving forward-backward, right-left and up-down. With the advent of the theory of relativity, we now understand time as an additional dimension. We can move though time as well and very importantly it is relative, it changes with speed and gravity. This describes the space-time continuum most general folks recognize today. Of relevant interest is work done by Ramban Nachmanides in the 13th century. Over 800 years ago, Nachmanides, one of three of the most venerated Hebrew rabbis' recognized from the first chapter of Genesis that the ten times it is written "and God said" that these 10 unction's implied 10 "man - measures" or we would say "dimensions" to the universe. [176] He described 4 as knowable and 6 as unknowable. Jewish nuclear physicists Gerald Schroder points out this startling fact in his work "Genesis and the Big Bang." [177]

In the 11th Century, Nachmanides declared from the scriptures that the universe had 10 dimensions, 900 years later, the superstring theory of quantum physics declares to us a 10 dimensional universe.

Before we get too far, let's summarize what we know from the scriptures. The universe, the time-space continuum is at least 4 dimensions and possibly 10 dimensions in its reality. Scripture has declared since the beginning the multidimensional aspect of the universe and a 10 dimensional view was developed about 900 years ago. Enter, advanced quantum physics and string theory. The most prevalent view among leading physicists today concerning the theory of physics and the universe is "Superstring" theory. Superstring theory teaches us that there are 10 if not more dimensions to the universe. Superstring theories are about 20 years old now. Looks like Nachmanides of the 11th century got there first, but he used the scriptures.

Background of the development of "Superstring Theory":
[178]

Einstein's theories of relativity (developed in the early 1900's) introduced the necessity of additional dimensions to the universe, time itself being an additional one and has been confirmed in 14 ways to 19 decimals. In the 1950's, Kaluza and Klein in following up on the general theory of relativity and incorporating the Lorentz symmetry to account for "ripples" in space-time, proposed adding a fourth spatial dimension, giving a total of five. However,

---

[176] "Ramban - Commentary on the Torah – Genesis"; Ramban Nachmanides; written in the13[th] Century; Translated by Rabbi Charles Chavel; Shilo Pub House Inc; copyright 1999; page 21

[177] "Genesis and the Big Bang"; Gerald Schroeder; Bantam Books; copyright 1990; page 59

[178] Background on "superstring theory" can be obtained from several places on the web. This information was extracted from an article by Steven Abel of the Centre for Theoretical Physics, University of Sussex, Brighton; see: http://physicsweb.org/articles/world/13/11/9

the Kluza-Klein theory had several critical weaknesses including the fact that it could not explain why the strength of the electromagnetic force is quite large while the gravitational force is fantastically weak.

Various "String Theories" began to emerge in the 1970's which included the addition of multiple dimensions and automatically included gravity. In the 1980's Michael Green and John Schwarz combined Supersymetry theories with String Theory developing "Superstring Theory." Superstring theory rather successfully incorporates quantum mechanics providing for a 10 dimensional universe, four of which we recognize as our usual 3D plus time and incorporating 6 additional dimensions that are tightly rolled or compacted similar to the old Kaluza-Klein theory.

In the late 1990's various "brane" theories began to be described which provide better results than previous models. It is also interesting that the "brane" theory gives us the understanding that the 4th dimension of our space-time continuum is incredibly thin. It is estimated to be about 10^{-15} mm (that is 10 with 15 zeros in front of it - which is about 100times smaller than the nucleus of an atom). A further and extremely shocking insight is that the theory also can account for the fact that nearly 95% of the matter in the universe is invisible (which is a disturbing fact in itself), but that is a subject for another time.

"bane" theories developed in the past 10 years of advanced quantum physics indicate that in the 4th physical dimension, the universe is very thin, perhaps only 10^{-15} mm thick which is about 100 times smaller than the nucleus of an atom!

Impact of Hyperspace:

The impact on our understanding using a hyperspace model is astounding. Secular scientists have stated the impact of a multidimensional universe. As an example of secular thinking, consider that following; "People found that the ramifications of the existence of higher dimensions were astounding. If you could manipulate the fourth or higher dimensions you would have god-like powers. [179]

- You could walk in such a way that no wall could stop you.
- You would appear to others to be passing through walls or doors.
- When hungry you could simply reach into the refrigerator, without opening the door.
- You could extract a section of an orange without peeling it.
- You could do surgery without cutting skin.
- You could disappear and reappear at will.
- You would be able to see people who had been buried by an avalanche."

---

[179] See: http://scholar.uwinnipeg.ca/courses/38/4500.6-001/Cosmology/dimensionality.htm

Visualizing Hyperspace:

Chuck Missler has stated that the only people who can visualize the 4th dimension are mathematicians and little children. Thinking it though, we will take a 1D to 2D to 3D to 4D development of an equally sided object.

Line	Square	Cube	Hypercube
—	□	(cube)	(hypercube)
1D	**2D**	**3D**	**4D**
Length = L	Area = LxL = L²	Volume =LxLxL=L³	Hyperspace =LxLxLxL=L⁴

What does this all mean to us?

Ephesians 6:12

[12] *"For our struggle is **not against flesh and blood**, but against the rulers, against the powers, against the world forces of this darkness, against the spiritual forces of wickedness **in the heavenly places**."*

Heavenly Places (Greek *epouranios*) definition: 1) existing in heaven (2) of heavenly origin or nature – Strong's #2032

Christians have been visualizing hyperspace from the beginning. It is often referred to as the **spiritual realm**. We know there are angels around us. They are among us when we pray and when we worship together in church. If they are in church, where are they? They are inside the building, we just can't see them. They are not ghosts or spirits, [180] that we could pass our hand

---

[180] There are evil spirits which do not posses a body, they seek a body (demon possession). They are fundamentally different from angels and fallen angels although most biblical scholars don't recognize the difference. Angels have bodies and can manifest themselves as a normal person and also in their radiance as seen by the shepherds to whom the angels appeared to announce the birth of Jesus. (Luke 2: 8-20)

through them. They are just a step back in the 4th dimension. They completely see into our 3D world we know but we don't accidentally bump into them. On occasion they step into our 3D world and we can see them just like they are a person. Consider the two angels who visited and brought destruction to Sodom and Gomorrah. They were mistaken for people. God tells us to treat strangers kindly because we do not know when we might entertain angels unaware. We know angels are around us and travel to the "Throne of God." If they travel there, distance must be involved. We will consider that in the next two sections.

Chapter 6.3

Heaven

2 Corinthians 12:2-4
*"I know a man in Christ who fourteen years ago-- whether in the body I do not know, or out of the body I do not know, God knows-- such a man was **caught up to the third heaven**. And I know how such a man-- whether in the body or apart from the body I do not know, God knows--was **caught up into Paradise**, and heard inexpressible words, which a man is not permitted to speak."* (NAS)

Where is heaven? Can you take a rocket ship there?

Is heaven part of our space-time continuum or is it somewhere else? If it is part of our universe, can we just get into a space ship and travel there? Looking carefully at Genesis chapter 1, we find that the heavens are indeed part of our universe.

Genesis 1:1 *"In the beginning **God created the heavens** and the earth."* (NAS)

Job 1:6-7 *"One day the angels came **to present themselves before the LORD**, and Satan also came with them. The LORD said to Satan, "Where have you come from?" Satan answered the LORD, "From roaming through the earth and going back and forth in it."* (NIV)

It is shocking to discover that Satan has access to the "Throne of God"!!!

Hebrews 12:22-24 *"But you have come to **Mount Zion and to the city of the living God, the heavenly Jerusalem**, and to myriads of angels, to the general assembly and church of the first-born who are enrolled in heaven, and to God, the Judge of all, and to the spirits of righteous men made perfect, and to Jesus, the mediator of a new covenant, and to the sprinkled blood, which speaks better than {the blood} of Abel."* (NAS)

I believe from Genesis 1 that heaven is indeed part of the time-space continuum or universe that we live in. From Hebrews, we see that there is a "heavenly" city of God.

Heavenly – Greek - *epouranios* (Strongs # 2032); above the sky:

6 - Hyperspace

From the Genesis account we can see that there are three heavens. [181]

- 1st Heaven – The air or atmosphere, our sky where the birds and airplanes fly (Gen 1:20, 26; Jer 4:25; Hag 1:10; Matt 8:20; 13:32; Acts 10:12; 14:17)

- 2nd Heaven – Is space or where the sun, moon and stars are located, where the astronauts fly (typically thought of as over 150,000 ft) (Gen 1:14-18; 22:17; 26:4; Matt 24:29; Heb 11:12; Rev 6:13)

- 3rd Heaven – Is the unseen world or the abode of God, where God dwells (2 Cor 12:1-4) – I'll suggest this is in hyperspace

Can we travel to the 3rd heaven in a spaceship? No, it is in hyperspace or the "spiritual" dimension. Jesus is there because He has His "resurrected" body, which is capable of traveling in hyperspace (see section 6.3.1) 6.6

How do we know it is really there? We have three witnesses to the fact of the existence of the spiritual heaven:

- 1st Paul – He was "caught up" to heaven where he received special revelation (2:Cor 12:1-4)

- 2nd John – He saw heaven (and a door) where he was shown the "things to come." (Rev 4:1-2)

- 3rd Jesus (Sufficient without the others) – He came from heaven and testifies of its existence (John 6:32-35)

Colossians 3:1-2 *"If then you have been raised up with Christ, keep seeking the **_things above, where Christ is_**, seated at the right hand of God. Set your mind on the things above, not on the things that are on earth."* (NAS)

From these verses, I suggest that:

- Heaven is a real place

- Jesus is currently in Heaven

- Heaven is "up" in that direction

- Heaven is part of our universe (space-time continuum)

- Heaven can not be reached via our normal three dimensions (up, back and across – [x, y, and z])

---

[181] References are from "The Footsteps of the Messiah"; Dr. Arnold Fruchtenbau; Ariel Ministries Pub; copyright 2003-2004; page 748

See the next chapter for a very bizarre biblical example of traveling in hyperspace.

6 - Hyperspace

Chapter 6.4

Traveling in Hyperspace - Example

Daniel 10:10-14
*"Then behold, a hand touched me and set me trembling on my hands and knees. And he said to me, "O Daniel, man of high esteem, understand the words that I am about to tell you and stand upright, **for I have now been sent to you**." And when he had spoken this word to me, I stood up trembling. Then he said to me, "Do not be afraid, Daniel, for **from the first day** that you set your heart on understanding this and on humbling yourself before your God, your words were heard, and **I have come** in response to your words. "**But the prince of the kingdom of Persia was withstanding me for twenty-one days**; then behold, Michael, one of the chief princes, came to help me, for I had been left there with the kings of Persia. "Now I have come to give you an understanding of what will happen to your people in the latter days, for the vision pertains to the days yet {future}."* (NAS)

What is going on here? Why can't an angel just travel where he wants to?

This is an absolutely fascinating story. Reading the entire passage reveals that Daniel, one of the greatest prophets of God, knew from prophecy that the time of captivity of his people Israel serving in Babylon was near complete. It was prophesied by Jeremiah (Daniel 9:2; Jer 25:11 and 2 Chr 36:21) to be 70 years. Daniel was interested in what was going to happen to the people in the future (Dan 10:14). So, at the time Daniel begins to pray for understanding, an angel is dispatched to bring the message to Daniel. Most shockingly, it takes **21 days** (Dan 10:13) for the angelic messenger to arrive. Even more reveling, the angel has to fight one of Satan's angelic beings (called the "Prince of Persia") to get through. Apparently, this "Prince" is stronger than the messenger angel is and the messenger has to call from help to get past the "Prince." Michael, the great archangel comes to the rescue to help our messenger get past. Re-stated, our angel, dispatched by God, travels through hyperspace to reach Daniel, but, on the way encounters a worker of Satan and engages in a battle, gets re-enforcement's and finally, after 21 days, is able to defeat the impeder and get through to Daniel. Wow!

189

6 - Hyperspace

This description beautifully describes to us what the "spiritual dimension" or hyperspace is like and gives us some amazing insights:

- Hyperspace is not just a "thin" dimension but has significant "depth" so that you can travel over a distance – There was some reasonable distance between the "Throne of God" where the angel was dispatched from and where Daniel was

- There is activity or "warfare" going on in this dimension – There was some type of struggle between the two angels

- There are geometric relationships between our normal "three dimensions" and that of hyperspace (a 4th dimension) – The angel couldn't just go to another place in hyperspace and appear to Daniel, he had to go to the place in hyperspace that was linked where Daniel was, that place was controlled by this enemy angel

This whole concept is difficult to grasp and comprehend. Although not quite exact, I'll suggest the following crude illustration that hopefully brings some clarification. Consider an example of a multi-story building; we live on the first floor, which corresponds, to our earth. We travel around on the "floor" and can even move (to some degree) up and down. There are however, floors above us. Imagine that the "Throne of God" is on the top floor. If an angel was to come from there (the upper floor) down to the earth (the lower floor) he would have to pass through the other floors. In the case of Daniel's angel, there was an enemy who was on the floor above Daniel and he blocked or prevented the angel from passing through.

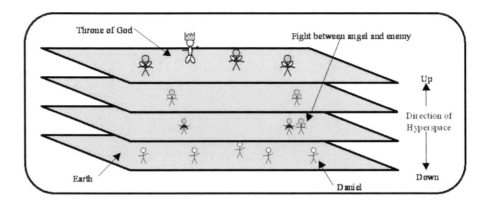

Crude illustration of traveling through hyperspace from the "Throne of God" to our earth's surface

6 - Hyperspace

Chapter 6.5

Breadth – Length – Depth - Height

Ephesians 3:17-19
"*[17]so that Christ may dwell in your hearts through faith; and that you, being rooted and grounded in love, [18]may be able to comprehend with all the saints what **is the breadth and length and height and depth**, [19]and to know the love of Christ which surpasses knowledge, that you may be filled up to all the fullness of God....*" (NAS)

Breadth (Greek - *platos*) Definition: breadth - suggesting great extent; Strong's #4114
Length (Greek – *mekos*) Definition: length; Strong's #3372
Depth (Greek - *bathos*)Definition: Depth or height; Strong's #899
Height (Greek – *hupsos*) Definition; height; Strong's #5311

The Price Paid:

We can not begin to really comprehend the Love of Christ for us. Some of what Jesus went through we read about. How he was brutalized and how He surrendered Himself and allowed Himself to be executed in a fashion that led to the creation and foundation of the word "excruciating", the highest level of pain that can be inflicted or experienced. How He descended into Hades and was 3 days in the belly of the earth. I have read many commentaries on what this all means and my personal opinion is that we can't begin to understand what Christ went through on our behalf. Many people have a glorious picture in their mind of what it will be like to "see" Christ for the first time when they get to heaven. Personally, I think that several of the passages that refer to Jesus in His post-resurrected state are frankly disturbing. They all suggest that what Isaiah prophesied about Him having been so extensively beaten so that He was no longer recognizable as a man might somehow be carried over into His resurrected state and the scars He will eternally bear on our behalf might be much more than just holes in His wrists and in His side. I'm not afraid of death (it's the dying I'm a little nervous about) and I am truly looking forward to going to heaven and all the things associated with it. I long to be with my Savior, but I don't think, however, that I am ready to see a brutalized Jesus. The price He had to pay for **my** sins ever evident in His broken body. I am afraid I might be repulsed at what I see. God forgive me!

The "Love of Christ...surpasses [our] knowledge" and we can not comprehend it in its entirety. So, to illustrate that fact, the Holy Spirit gives us the surprising insight that there are more to this universe that just the three dimensions (up, down and sideways). Just like we can not fully understand Christ's love for us, we have trouble understanding the additional dimensions of this universe.

Bye the bye: Israel, as a nation, is a prototype of the Messiah (as illustrated by Matthew who identified Jesus' coming out of Egypt as a fulfillment of prophecy) and Isaiah 51:22-23 (which proceeds not by coincidence chapter 53 – the crucifixion) describes the restoration of Israel and we find that the nations who oppressed Israel will be punished. As example, God brought Babylon as a form of judgment upon the Israelites, however, because of their brutality, which was unnecessary, they are accountable. Likewise, it was unnecessary for Jesus, who came specifically to die for our sins, to be brutalized. Those responsible will be held accountable and time has not mitigated the seriousness of their offence.

Implication of 4 Dimensions:

As a young engineer this verse was very disturbing to me. I worked in just three dimensions and to see Christ's love described in four didn't sit well with me. As I learned more, however, I began to see the universe in terms of "hyperspace", a multi-dimensional space-time continuum. I always knew the spiritual world was real and "out there" but it wasn't until I learned advanced physics was I able to link the two. This verse now says to me; "there is much more to My love for you than what you can comprehend through earthly eyes, it has deep spiritual dimensions beyond your capacity to understand." Halleluiah!

Chuck Missler: "One of the many advantages that 20th century science has given us is that, thanks to Dr. Albert Einstein's brilliant discoveries, we now know that time is a physical property and is subject to mass, acceleration, and gravity. We have come to realize that we live in a four-dimensional continuum properly known as "space-time." (This is what Paul seems to imply in his letter to the Ephesians 3:18) It is interesting that when one takes the apparent 10^{12} expansion factor involved in the theories of the "expanding universe," that an assumed 16 billion years reduce to six days!" [182]

---

[182] http://www.khouse.org/articles/2003/492/

6 - Hyperspace

Chapter 6.6

Resurrected Body in Hyperspace

Luke 24:31
"*...and their eyes were opened and they recognized Him [Jesus – the Christ]; and **He vanished from their sight**"* (NAS)

Jesus vanishes from plain sight! Don't let your familiarity with this passage cause you to miss something deeper!

Vanished (translated from two Greek words "*ginomai*" – Strong's #1096 and "*aphantos*" – Strong's #855
- "*Ginomai*" definition: to cause to be; i.e. to become
- "*Aphantos*" definition: non-manifested; i.e. invisible

Wow! Is Jesus a magician doing a disappearing act to impress everyone? Or perhaps Jesus is now the invisible man. Be careful, you might accidentally bump into him.   May be he was "beamed" up like a "Star Trek" type transporter. According to the text, Jesus was there one moment, and "zap" the next moment the was gone. He vanished? My question is, "Where did He go?" I think the Holy Spirit has several messages for us to learn from these passages. We can perhaps gain insight into the capabilities of Jesus and His "resurrected" body. Turns out it can do some pretty amazing things. Also of interest to us, we too (those who have been "born again" – John 3:3, 7; 1Peter 1:3, 23) will one day receive our resurrected body and it will possess the same amazing and exciting characteristics that Christ's body does.

> **Several million Jews were crucified or killed during the Roman occupation of Israel, but only one rose from the dead**

First, we will address this "vanishing" capability. There are several options that could describe what happened to Jesus when He disappeared. They are briefly summarized here:
- Invisible Man: He became "transparent" to us like glass. You can see through Him, don't know he is there unless you reach out and touch

Him. (May be we should run around throwing paint in the air in hopes of catching Him and then we can see Him) This concept seems unlikely because the passage seems to indicate that He left, not that He was there and you couldn't see Him. He doesn't start talking while no one sees Him. (However – Paul's conversion is Acts is interesting in that the manifestation was a "bright light" but I will leave this for another time)

- Beamed Up: It could be conceived that, like in the "Star Trek" series, there is a "transporter" which basically breaks down all you molecules, shoots them across space, and then recombines them again. Vincent Price went through this in the old science thriller "The Fly" where he is transported over the phone lines to another location. One problem. Fly went into the transporter. Bummer. Price comes out at the other end with a man's body but with the head of a fly (how the fly's head got big really isn't explained) but what I thought was really cool was the fly's body that got Price's human head. Little fly buzzing around with a miniature human head talking in squeaky high voice. Now that was cool, too bad he got stuck in that spiders web, real bummer. Anyway, I got side tracked. There seems to be no indication in the Scriptural text of a transporter so I'll leave this as less likely as well.

- Ghost: It's Casper the friendly ghost. He has shown up but because he is a spirit, some time you see him and sometimes you don't. I don't think this is it because the scriptures tell us that the people could "touch" Him. A spirit or ghost can't be touched, you would pass your hand right through it.

- Hyperspace: Potentially Jesus just "moved" in the direction we can't see. As the section of Hyperspace has illustrated, there are additional dimensions to the normal three (front to back, side to side, and up and down) that we are limited to with our "earthly" bodies. If Jesus, with His resurrected or "Heavenly" body (1 Cor 15:42-44) can move in the other dimensions of Hyperspace, we would expect Him to be able to "appear" and "disappear" from thin air. I think this is a more likely possibility for understanding what is taking place.

Imagine that if there are angels present with us in a room, but we can't see them, where are they? There are really there but just standing back slightly in Hyperspace. We can't see them because we can't see in that "direction." I'll call it the "spiritual" direction. That is not meant to say it is any less real than our physical dimension. In fact, we will find out that reality really becomes clearer and more distinct with all dimensions included. The spiritual dimension is not a place of the mind or thought, it is a real place, tangible and of substance with 4 or more directional dimensions. Given the ability to travel into that dimension, you would find truer, clearer, of more substance than our three dimensional world we understand. Using a comparison of 2D verses 3D we can illustrate the situation.

Imagine a world that lives on a piece of paper. Flat objects, of all sizes and shapes, triangles, squares, circles can move around in this flat 2D space. If we constructed a square with a door, objects could move in the plane of the paper into the box and out of the box if the door was open. If the door was closed, objects would be unable to move into the square. However, if we now use the 3rd dimension and pick up the triangle, we could place it into the square without ever having to open the door. If a triangle, which is normally confined to travel only in the plane of the paper, is now free to move in the additional 3rd dimension, it could do things that would absolutely amaze it's little 2d friends. In the same fashion, we are limited to movement in our 3d space, but if perhaps we received the ability to move in an additional 4th dimension (not time as the 4th) we would be able to "appear" and "vanish" before our little 3D friends.

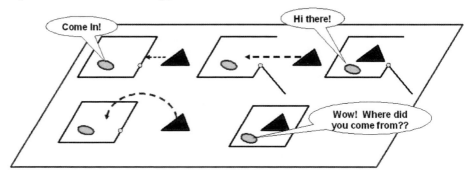

2D objects moving in a 2D plane are limited – a 2D object moving in 3D seems miraculous to his 2D friends

As "off the wall" and "bizarre" is some of my thinking, we find this same thought reflected by secular scientists. As noted on the "Winnipeg" information site in the cosmology section, they note the conjectures put forth by Bernhard Riemann in 1854 about multiple dimensions which is now referred to as "hyperspace." As mention in the section on Hyperspace, most physicists of today support the "String Theory" of quantum mechanics which states that the universe is 10 plus dimensions. Winnipeg notes:
"Riemann's ideas started many people thinking about higher dimensions. People found that the ramifications of the existence of higher dimensions were astounding. If you could manipulate the fourth or higher dimensions you would have god-like powers.

- You could walk in such a way that no wall could stop you.
- You would appear to others to be passing through walls or doors.
- When hungry you could simply reach into the refrigerator, without opening the door.
- You could extract a section of an orange without peeling it.
- You could do surgery without cutting skin.
- You could disappear and reappear at will.
- You would be able to see people who had been buried by an avalanche." [183]

It is important to note, that when we receive our resurrected or heavenly bodies, they will be like Christ's body in that multi-dimensional sense. Just as when Christ was upon the earth originally, our bodies were like His. In the future, our body will be like His as well. That doesn't mean we become gods. Jesus, as God, "emptied" Himself and took on human form (Phil 2:6-8), God in the flesh (John 1 "and the Word [Son of God] became flesh and dwelt among us" – John 1:14). Jesus now after His crucifixion has been raised up with a new "resurrected body." 1 Corinthians 15 tells us that our bodies will are sown as perishable (that means we will die and be "planted" into the ground) but will be raised imperishable meaning everlasting. We get a new body, an eternal body, a tangible 4 plus dimensional body, like the one Christ modeled for us, but we do not become a god. Only God is God (Father, Son and Holy Spirit), and we will always be man, however, a much more capable and dynamic man.

As 1 Corinthians 15: says:

[42] *"So will it be with the resurrection of the dead. The body that is sown is perishable, it is raised imperishable;* [43]*it is sown in dishonor, it is raised in glory; it is sown in weakness, it is raised in power;* [44]*it is sown a natural body, it is raised a spiritual body. If there is a natural body, there is also a spiritual body....* [50] *"I declare to you, brothers, that flesh and blood cannot inherit the kingdom of God, nor does the perishable inherit the imperishable......* [53]*For the perishable must clothe itself with the imperishable, and the mortal with immortality.* [54]*When the perishable has been clothed with the imperishable, and the mortal with immortality, then the saying that is written will come true:*

---

[183] http://scholar.uwinnipeg.ca/courses/38/4500.6-001/Cosmology/dimensionality.htm

"Death has been swallowed up in victory."
55"Where, O death, is your victory?
Where, O death, is your sting?"

Other Characteristics of our "Resurrected Bodies"

Jesus made 11 appearances with His resurrected body appearing to crowds as large as 500 people that were noted in the scriptures.   Christ and His resurrection is a keystone to the Christian faith and that unique and singular fact separates His followers from those of other religions.   The table below indicates the scriptural accounts in apparent chronological order.

Event	Matt	Mark	Luke	John	1 Cor	Reference	Event	Saw	Heard	Touched	Food Eaten	Other
1	1	1	1	1		Matt 28:1; Mark 16:1; Luke 24:1; John 20:1	Mary Magdalene & Mary (mother of James - Mark 16:1) visit the tomb & meet two (Luke 24:4) angels	X	X	X		Empty Tomb
2		2				Mark 16:9	Jesus appears first to Mary Magdalene	X	X	X		Empty Tomb
3	2			2		Matt 28:9; John 20:14	Jesus meets the two Marys on their way to the disciples	X	X	X		Empty Tomb
4		3	2			[Mark 16:12] Luke 24:13-32	Jesus appeared to two walking in the country (Sunday - after the women visit the tomb - Luke 24:13,22) Jesus breaks bread with them (Luke 24:30)	X	X		Bread	
5			3		1	Luke 24:34; I Cor 15:5	Jesus appears to Simon (Peter) - referenced	X	X			Empty Tomb; clothes
6			3	2	2	Luke 24:36; John 20:19-23; 1 Cor 15:5	Jesus appears to the ten (Thomas missing) in the evening of the first day (John 20:19) (Jerusalem - Luke 24:33) as they were eating; Jesus asks for something to eat and has broiled fish (Luke 24:41)	X	X	X*	Broiled Fish	Saw Wounds
7		4		4		John 20:24; [Mark 16:14]	Jesus meets with the disciples and Thomas a week after the previous visit	X	X	X*		Saw Wounds
8	3			5		John 21:1; {Matt 28:16-20} Acts 1:4	Jesus meets the disciples by the Sea of Galilee, they have bread and fish (3rd visit by Jesus to the disciples) Jesus meets the disciples at a mountain in Galilee Jesus eats with them and tells them to stay in Jerusalem (Acts 1:4)	X	X		Bread and Fish	
9					3	1 Cor 15:6	Appears to more than 500 brothers in Christ	X	X			
10					4	1 Cor 15:7	Appears to James (Brother ?)	X	X			
11		5	4			Luke 24:50; Acts 1:4-9; [Mark 16:19]	They go to Bethany (Luke 24:50) where he is taken up into heaven and became hidden by a cloud (Acts 1:9) Two men appear (Acts 1:10)	X	X			

* Offered him self for touching

Post resurrection recorded appearances of Jesus

There are other characteristics of the resurrected body I find provocative. Not only could Jesus move in the 4th dimension "appearing" and "disappearing", He went through a wall as well. Because He is tangible, not a spirit, people could touch and hold Him. A fascinating characteristic of our resurrected body is that we can eat. That is surprising. I'll suggest that because the scriptures tell us that our body is eternal (1John 5:13) it is not necessary for us to eat to sustain life, but apparently, it is a pleasure or capability. Fantastic, eat without worrying about gaining weight. I'm looking forward to that. Jesus modeled this several times by eating fish and also noted at the last supper that He would drink wine again when we finally were joined with Him. Fabulous, I'm looking forward to that as well.

Characteristic	Ref
Saw Him	Matt; Mark 16:12 & Others
Appeared in a different Form	Mark 16:12
Took hold of His feet	Matt 28:9
Touch Him	Luke 24:39
Mary grabs ahold of Him	John 20:17
Spoke - Gave them instructions	Matt 28:10; Luke 24:46 & Others
Appears in a closed room	John 20:19
Appears in a closed room	John 20:26
He stands in their midst - Appears from out of "thin air"	Luke 24:36
He vanishes from plain sight	Luke 24:31
He eats broiled fish	Luke 24:42
Jesus eats bread and fish	John 20:12

Demonstrated characteristics of Christ's resurrected body

Luke 24:40-
"And when He had said this, He showed them His hands and His feet. And while they still could not believe it for joy and were marveling, He said to them, "Have you anything here to eat?"" And they gave Him a piece of a broiled fish; and He took it and ate it before them." Let me set this up from the disciple's point of view. After going through the trauma of the crucifixion day, after losing all hope that Jesus would overthrow the Romans and He is now dead, some of the women begin to claim they have seen Jesus alive. Jesus then appears out of thin air into a closed room. They are shocked and frighten out of their wits. After Jesus demonstrates the fact that He is real and not a spirit

or ghost, He says; "by the way, you guys have any food?" There is so much I don't understand.

1 John 3:2
"*Beloved, now we are children of God, and it has not appeared as yet what we will be.* ___We know that when He appears, we will be like Him___, *because we will see Him just as He is.*"

Congratulations – You have just entered Hyperspace!!!

6 - Hyperspace

Chapter 6.7

Pre-existent Christ

John 8:57-59a
*"Then said the Jews unto him, Thou art not yet fifty years old, and hast thou seen Abraham? Jesus said unto them, Verily, verily, I say unto you, **Before Abraham was, I am**. Then took they up stones to cast at him"* (KJV)

John 1:1-3
*"¹In the beginning was the Word, and the Word was with God, and the Word was God. ²**He was in the beginning with God. ³All things came into being through Him, and apart from Him nothing came into being that has come into being**. ..."* (NAS)

John 1:14
*14 "**And the Word became flesh**, and dwelt among us, and we saw His glory, glory as of the only begotten from the Father, full of grace and truth"*

Pre-Existent Christ

Some folks seem to think that Jesus was just a "man." Scriptures indicate that indeed he was/is 100% man but there's a lot more to the story. Jesus is also God, 100% God who pre-existed the formation of the universe. In fact, Jesus made the universe, the time-space continuum we now live in. Because he made it, it also means that He pre-existed time, being that time was created and started at the creation of Genesis 1:1. So what was before that, at T minus something? That would be eternity past (see section 3.1 for more explanation), but what I would like to point out here is that clearly, Jesus the Christ, our Lord and Savior was God, before the beginning.

The Great "I AM" – Voice of the Burning Bush

At the age of 80, after 40 years as a very senior leader in Pharaoh's court followed by 40 years as a shepherd, Moses was called by God to lead the deliverance of Israel from slavery in Egypt. From what would appear to be one of the strangest of places to receive a call from, God chose a bush that was burning but not consumed. Our Hebrew Rabbi friends will tell us that Moses just didn't turn out of curiosity, but what is meant by turning to the bush is: as you decide to turn and approach the bush, you know this is a major turning point in your life, a defining moment and you will never be the same again. It was such an event for Moses, a defining point in his life.

Anyway, in the conversation between God and Moses, Moses wants to clarify the name of the God of his fathers to eliminate confusion when he confronts the Israelites. God simply responds: *"God said to Moses, "I AM WHO I AM"; and He said, "Thus you shall say to the sons of Israel, 'I AM has sent me to you."'* (Ex 3:14) "I Am" is one of the names of God. "I Am" is the voice of the burning bush. So, exactly who is the "I Am?" God for sure but who, the Father, Son or Holy Spirit? It appears that Jesus informs us that He is the "I Am." This is clear for John 8:59 when in discussion with the Pharisees, Jesus makes the point. Jesus said before Abraham was, "I Am", and in case we missed it the Pharisees clarify by taking up stones to stone Him because they understood He was claiming to be God, the voice of the burning bush. Later in John 18:5-6: "Jesus saith unto them, I am [he]. ...As soon then as he had said unto them, I am [he], they went backward, and fell to the ground." The "he" in the verse is not really there, it has been added. What Jesus really said was "I Am" the voice of the burning bush, and when he said this, they fell to the ground. Tip: when you meet the God of the universe, get on your knees.

Chapter 6.8

Mass-less Soul

1 Corinthians 2:12
"Now we have received, not the spirit of the world, but the Spirit who is from God, that we might know the things freely given to us by God."

John 6:63
"It is the Spirit who gives life, the flesh profits nothing, the words that I [Jesus] have spoken to you are spirit and are life."

John 4:24
"God is spirit, and those who worship Him must worship in spirit and truth."

No Mass – No Limitations

In kind of a backwards way, you can prove that there is a soul as part of a human and that his soul is eternal. The proof kind of goes like this:

- What makes you you? Your personality, your individuality and all those associated things are you, your life. There is more to you than just an arrangement of chemical compositions.
- That "you", your life that is in you, departs your body when you die.
- When you die and your soul/spirit departs there is no change in the weight (mass) of you body. If we were to weigh the body just before death and then immediately after death, it would weigh the same.
- Therefore: your soul/spirit has no mass (weight)

Now, coming at things from the physics point of view:
- Einstein has shown us that time is relative, it varies with gravity and speed.
- All objects of mass are subject to laws of physics, including time; however, things of no mass are not subject to time or degradation as experienced by the entropy laws.
- Therefore; by definition, mass-less things are eternal
- Therefore; your spirit/soul are eternal.

Perhaps an analogy will clarify. Consider a blank Compact Disk (CD). It has no information on it but has a certain weight. If you load that blank CD into your CD burner on your computer, you can store all kinds of information. Over 650 mega bites of software and data. In fact, you can have all kinds of programs loaded on the CD that can operate you computer. When this CD is fully loaded, it still weighs the same as it did when it was empty. The software weighs nothing. The CD is just the physical carrier of the software. In the same way, we are first and foremost, soul and spirit, software. I just purchased a new computer to replace my old 6-year-old machine. I spent the evening moving all my files off the old and onto the new. I have now everything that I had before but now with a great big color flat screen. Programs run amazingly fast and I can store and add much more information than ever before. You and I are headed for an upgrade. One day our old bodies will be cast aside and we will inherit our new, resurrected hyperspace bodies. Our soul and our spirit are software, they will be uploaded to our new bodies.

Atheist Clarifies:

Frank Tipler, a professor of Mathematical Physics at Tulane University, who is a major theoretician in the field of global general relativity, the rarefied

> *"For God so loved the world that He gave His only Son, that whosoever believes in Him, should not perish but have everlasting life."* John 3:16

branch of physics created by Stephen Hawking and Roger Penrose, was an atheist. "However, in devising a mathematical model of the end of the universe, Tipler came to a stunning conclusion: Using the most advanced and sophisticated methods of modern physics, relying solely on the rigorous procedures of logic that science demands, he had created a proof of the existence of God." [184]

Using the laws of physics and relativity Tipler came to a number of startling conclusions:

- There is a God (see cover of his book)
- The Laws of Physics and the universal boundary conditions necessarily permit life to continue to exist forever, proving the Eternal Life Postulate (see page 213 of his book)
- It is inevitable that there will be a resurrection of all dead at the "end".
- The resurrection body could be vastly improved over our current bodies (page 242 of his book)

---

[184] "Physics of Immortality"; Frank Tipler; Double Day Pub; copyright 1994 – see front flap

Even though I don't agree with much of where Tipler takes his conclusions, it is provocative that an atheist, using physics can demonstrate the existence of the spiritual realm, the resurrection of the soul and its associated eternal life.

The Scriptures have declared to us these same principles for over 3,500 years.
God is Real
"In the beginning God created the heavens and the earth"; God existed prior to the beginning of our time-space continuum (Genesis 1:1)

All will be resurrected - All souls are eternal
"So also is the resurrection of the dead. It is sown a perishable body, it is raised an imperishable body, it is sown in dishonor, it is raised in glory, it is sown in weakness, it is raised in power; it is sown a natural body, it is raised a spiritual body. So also it is written, 'The first man, Adam, became a living soul.' The last Adam became a life-giving spirit." (1 Cor 15:15)

Even those who follow Satan and the "Beast" will be resurrected for eternal judgment.
"The rest of the dead did not come to life until the thousand years were completed. This is the first resurrection." (Rev 20:5)

> "*What good will it be for a man if he gains the whole world, yet forfeits his soul? Or what can a man give in exchange for his soul?*"
> Matthew 16:26

6 - Hyperspace

Chapter 6.9

View Across Time

Overview

Verses

Matt 4:8-10 "Again, the devil took Him to a very high mountain, and showed Him all the kingdoms of the world, and their glory; and he said to Him, "All these things will I give You, if You fall down and worship me." Then Jesus said to him, "Be gone, Satan! For it is written, 'You shall worship the Lord your God, and serve Him only.'" (NAS)

Luke 4:5-8 "And he led Him up and showed Him all the kingdoms of the world in a moment of time. And the devil said to Him, "I will give You all this domain and its glory; for it has been handed over to me, and I give it to whomever I wish. "Therefore if You worship before me, it shall all be Yours." And Jesus answered and said to him, "It is written, 'You shall worship the Lord your God and serve Him only.'" (NAS)

Words:

⇨ Mountain (Greek *Oros* - Strong's 3735 – 63x)
  • First use in New Testament is here (Matt 4:8)
  • Same word used in Heb 12:8 which refers to heavenly Mt. Zion
⇨ Kingdom (Greek *basileia* Strong's 932 = Kingdom, sovereignty, royal power – 163x)
⇨ World – different words are used in the two passages
  • Matt 4:8 World ~ Greek *kosmos* – Strong's 2889 = order of the world, the ordered universe, then the abode of humanity[185] – 186x
  • Luke 4:5 World ~ Greek *oikoumene* – Strong's 3625 = inhabited earth – 15x
⇨ Domain (Greek *exousia* – Strong's 1849 = power to act, authority – 91x)
⇨ Moment (Greek *Stigme* – Strong's 4743 = a point of time, ie and instant – 1x)
  • Word used only once in the Bible (others are 1824 *exautes* 6x; 5610 *hora* 106x and 823 *atomos* 1x)
⇨ Time (Greek *chronos* – Strong's 5550 = a space of time or interval – 54x)

---

[185] "A Critical Lexicon and Concordance to the English and Greek New Testament"; E.W. Bullinger; Kregel Pub.; origionally pub 1908; Kregel Pub 1999; page 900

- There are several other words translated "time"

Verbs in Matthew 4:8 (verse 8 "**took** Him to a very high mountain" and "**showed** Him all the kingdoms") are present tense in the Greek. According to NAS present tense is used for historical events for emphasis. The direct words actually would state "the devil takes Him to a very high mountain, and shows Him…"[186]

Heb 12:22 "But you have come to Mount Zion and to the city of the living God, the heavenly Jerusalem, and to myriads of angels," (NAS)

"Notice that Luke's account reverses the order of the second and third temptations as recorded in Matthew. The word "then" in Matthew 4:5 seems to indicate sequence thus being the one chronologically ordered. [187] "The order in Luke corresponds to the nature of man. Man is composed of Body, Soul and Spirit. The first temptation concerns the body; the second the soul, and the third the spirit." [188]

Where was Jesus taken?

This appears to be a statement of moving into other dimensions of space. This thought is supported by the reference to "moment" used only once in the Bible. This is not figurative, it is literal. By the way, you can't see very far from 10,000' or even 30,000.' Even from an airplane at 35,000' you can't see multiple states let alone the nations of the world.

---

[186] "New American Standard Bible"; Lockman Foundation; Foundation Press; copyright 1960, 1973;

[187] The Bible Exposition Commentary – New Testament Vol 1"; Warren Wiersbe: Victor; Cook Communications; copyright 2001, first printed 1989; page 19

[188] "The Annotated Bible – New Testament Vol 1"; A.C. Gaebelein; Our Hope Pub; copyright 1913; page 135

Chapter 6.10

1,500 Mile High Jerusalem

Overview

Verses

Revelation 21:16 *"And the city is laid out as a square, and its length is as great as the width; and he measured the city with the rod fifteen hundred miles; its length and width **and height** are equal."* (NAS)

Our eventual home promises to be an absolutely awesome place. Even though we only have brief, sketchy information, Revelation 21 communicates to us a fascinating, amazingly and beautiful vision of some of its characteristics. Examples include walls over 200 feet high, massive gates made of a single pearl, gold city and streets of pure gold like transparent glass. We are also told the dimensions of this city. It is 1,500 miles by 1,500 miles by 1,500 miles. Imagine a city that is more than 2/3's the size of the continental United States. The largest city ever, but what about it's height? It is 1,500 miles high! Lets slow down a minute; herein lies a difficulty.

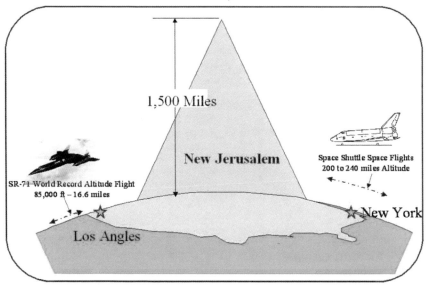

1,500 Miles

New Jerusalem

SR-71 World Record Altitude Flight
85,000 ft – 16.6 miles

Space Shuttle Space Flights
200 to 240 miles Altitude

New York

Los Angles

1,500 miles is way out there! Mount Everest is just over 30,000 feet which is less than 6 miles. The SR-71 stealth aircraft which set the sustained flight high altitude record near the edge of space at just over 85,000 feet is an incredible 16 miles high. Space Shuttle orbits are typically about 220 miles high, clearly in space. If New Jerusalem is over 1,500 miles high in our 3 dimensional coordinate system, we will encounter several problems. First, there is no atmosphere. Because followers of God during this age of history will have resurrected bodies similar to the one modeled by Jesus when He rose from the grave, breathing an oxygen atmosphere might not be an issue. However, earth's spin dynamics will be. Earth is spin stabilized, which means that its rotation keeps it oriented on it's rotation axis, ie. day is consistent, and seasons are consistent. If there is a large mountainous city on the side of the earth (assuming that earth is similar in size as to what it is today) it would cause a significant wobble. A top spins smoothly as long as it is "balanced." If it is not balanced, it would rotate in a very wobbly fashion (consider the vibration in a car when even one wheel is slightly out of balance). New Jerusalem is significant enough in size to cause a major instability in earth's rotation.

So, what is going on here? I can see three potential solutions:

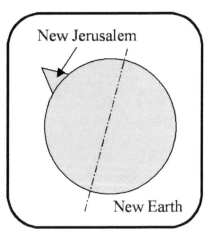

- ♦ (1) The dimensions are allegorical or metaphorical and not "real" dimensions of a city – I don't think this is true primarily because the following verse, Revelation 21:17 makes a point to tell us these are "human measurements, which are also angelic measurements" clearly stating these are not symbolic in any sense.
- ♦ (2) All three dimensions (length, width and height) are straightforward in our 3 dimensional understanding. This would be consistent with the biblical text however, because of the physics and dynamics problems stated above, it seems unlikely to me.
- ♦ (3) One or more of the dimensions are in another dimensional direction from that of our standard 3D. It is a hyperspace dimension. With the 10 dimensional universe recognized in "string theory" of quantum physics of today, the height dimension could potentially be different from what we normally would suspect. I believe this is a very likely solution based of the explanation, which follows.

Words:

The Greek word for height is "*hupsos*" and it is only used 5 times in scripture [being translated to height (2x); high (3x) and high position (1x). In one of these references (Eph 3:18) it is to a description of comprehension of Christ's love for us where the illustration is made to it's (1) breath, (2) length, (3) height, and (4) depth. Four dimensions, clearly beyond our normal 3D world (although this is a simile example). Another example is Eph 4:8 where it states that our Resurrected Lord "ascended on high [hupsos]" speaking of going to heaven. Provocative! This creates a possibility that the "height" of Revelation could be the same as the "high" of Heaven, which Christ ascended to. It is pointed out in the "Dictionary of New Testament Theology – Vol 2" that; "Used absolutely, *hypsos* often denotes the heavenly realm."[189] The Septuagint version of the Old Testament of Psalm 68:19 "ascended on high" translated the word "high" into the same Greek word *hupsos*.

Our second reason for considering "height" in the hyperspace direction is the reference in Revelation 21:17 where it equates "human" and "angelic" measurements. The "angelic" realm is clearly part of hyperspace and not of the normal 3D world perceived by our physical senses. This clearly creates the possibility of hyperspace from the passage.

The biblical Greek text uses the word "*stadion*" [Strongs 4712][190] and the measurement is 12,000 "*stadion*." A *stadion* according to Ungers bible dictionary is 606.75 feet [191] and would actually make 1,200 *stadion* a little over 1,300 miles.

---

[189] "New International Dictionary of New Testament Theology – Vol 2"; Colin Brown General Editor; Zondervan; copyright 1967-1986; page 199

[190] "Zondervan NASB Exhaustive Concordance"; Zondervan; copyright 1981 and 1998; page 1566

[191] "Ungers Bible Dictionary"; Electronic version; PC Study Bible – Reference Library Plus – Version 2; METROLOGY

6 - Hyperspace

Chapter 6.11

Population and Real Estate in Heaven

Overview

Verses
Revelation 21:16 *"And the city is laid out as a square, and its length is as great as the width; and he measured the city with the rod fifteen hundred miles; its length and width **and height** are equal."* (NAS)

Moving to a new home is one of the more exciting and, at the same time, more stressful times in our lives. Our Lord stated that He is in the process of preparing a place for us (John 14:3)[192] with the understanding that this will be our home in the future. What will this be like? How will this work? Limited information is provided to us to help answer these questions so our understanding will only be so deep, but let's take a look at a few things that are stated. One subject that we can address and make some estimates on is the area or size of land that we will have available for new homes. We will address this by taking a look at the problem from two perspectives. The first involves normal 3 dimensional thinking and the second will involve an understanding of hyperspace as described in the previous section. To determine what will be available to us, we will first make an estimate of the anticipated number of people (referred to as souls) and then compare that with anticipated available land area (both current and in hyperspace).

A reasonable estimate of the number of souls that are anticipated to be in heaven is developed from world population statistics and a guess as to the percentage of "saved" people. World population over time is subject to speculation but for this exercise, publish secular estimates will be used in combination with Christian estimates of world population around the time of Noah's flood. The adjoining table shows the world population estimates, estimates for average life span, and the combined results for cumulative

---

[192] John 14:2-3 "In My Father's house are many dwelling places; if it were not so, I would have told you; for I go to prepare a place for you. "And if I go and prepare a place for you, I will come again, and receive you to Myself; that where I am, {there} you may be also." (NAS)

population. Cumulative population would be the total number of people born since Adam and Eve. The population estimates of the earth at the time of the flood vary widely ranging from several hundred thousand to over several billion. I assumed a nearly doubling of population every 50 years which resulted in as estimate of just 400 million people at the time of Noah's flood (It really wasn't Noah who caused the flood, I just refer to it by his name because he was the one who modeled salvation from judgment via the ark) [193].

Date	World Pop. (M)	Avg. Life Span (yr)	Cumulative People Born (M)	Cumulative Heavenly Souls (M)
4,000 BC	0	300	0.0	0.0
3,500 BC	0.2	300	0.3	0.0
3,000 BC	2	300	3.8	0.6
2,500 BC	438	100	2,193	329
2,000 BC	2	50	2,213	332
1,500 BC	26	50	2,473	371
1,000 BC	50	50	2,973	446
500 BC	75	50	3,723	558
0	170	50	5,423	813
500 AD	190	50	7,323	1,098
1,000 AD	254	50	9,863	1,479
1,500 AD	425	50	14,113	2,117
2,000 AD	6,082	60	64,797	9,719

A very difficult number to estimate but very leveraging when determining the number of souls anticipated to be in heaven is: "what percentage of the population came to saving faith?" To make this estimate, I used the words of Jesus when He stated in Matt 7:13-14; "Enter by the narrow gate; for the gate is wide, and the way is broad that leads to destruction, and many are those who enter by it. For the gate is small, and the way is narrow that leads to life, and

---

[193] Noah and his family were saved by the "Ark." The focal point within the Temple of God, we find the "Ark of the Covenant." Not only is the "Ark of the Covenant" representative of God and His presence, but is also an illustrative reference to Jesus being the "Ark of our salvation" which links all these things together in a typological illustrative manner. The "Ark of the Covenant" being make of wood (or organic referring to Christ in human bodily form) and is covered with gold (Exodus 25:10-15) (representative of Christ purity and holiness as God).

few are those who find it." (NAS) Narrow is defined as "small in width; not wide" [194] so I used a guess of 15%. These statistics and estimates result in an estimated nearly 65 billion people who have been born on this earth and a "saved" population of just under 10 billion souls (it is interesting to compare that number with today's population of about 6.5 billion). It is also interesting to note that the number of "saved" Jews up to the time of Christ is 813 million. Recognizing that the saved people since Christ's time are part of His body and would represent the nearly 10 billion minus the 813 million which results in a count just over 9 billion. An eternal ratio of Christians/Israelites would be about 9/1. We will use this factor when we consider the "New Jerusalem."

A friend asked the other day a great question. "How much space will we have in our eternal kingdom?" This is a fun concept to think through. We will first look at this in normal 3D space and then in hyperspace dimensions. Today's earth is 196,940,400 square miles in surface area. The oceans cover about 70 percent of the area leaving about 57 million square miles of land from which we subtract Antarctica (assuming no one wants to live in eternal winter) lakes and other obvious inhabitable areas resulting in about 45 million square miles of usable land (this does assume that this will be a similar number for the Millennial age). Now, watch this. If we have about 10 billion eternal life people, use only half of the 45 million square miles (leaving open space), we come out with about 1 ½ acres of land for each of us. An acre and a half! That's a lot of land! During the Millennium the earth will be cleaned upped and restored to it's "designed" condition, which will be perhaps similar to that of the Garden of Eden.

When we consider the "New Heaven" and "New Earth" of Revelation 19 & 20 we need to move into a thinking pattern of hyperspace as previously noted. Assuming that the New Earth is similar in size to our current earth, we could expect a similar land apportion. A reasonable thought is to consider that the "New Jerusalem" is designed for the Israelites and the Body of Christ will live in the remaining portion of the Earth. If the estimated number of "Saved Israelites" is 813 million as noted above, we place them in this new city of 1,500 miles by 1,500 miles, and assuming a city open space of about 25%, the result is about 1.3 acres per person. Again, that seems like a comfortable size for each home of one person. The rest of us, as Christ's Body, would have about the same 1.5 acres per person. This would seem ample in itself but to really understand what we will be given, we need to consider one more dimension, that of hyperspace.

---

[194] Webster's New World Dictionary"; Southwestern Company; 1966 edition; Page 496

6 - Hyperspace

As stated in the previous chapter, our new home is not just what we have here in 3D space, there is an additional dimension. One way to picture this is to think of a tall building with an elevator. The first floor would represent what we see in 3D space. Let's say there is a 2,000 square feet on this floor, which would be similar to many homes. But, there is a lot more to this building. We can travel up one floor in an elevator to the second story where we find a completely different room of another 2,000 square feet. We could continue to travel up and up to many other floors. Hyperspace can be crudely visualized in a similar fashion. We not only have the 1.5 acres on the first floor, we can move in a different direction to a completely new level (floor) were we have another, potentially completely different 1.5 acres. The amazing news is that we can continue to move to other floors in that direction where, in essence, we have additional space. How many "floors" do we own? Well, considering Rev 21:16 (see NIV version for direct translation) we have 12,000 stadia in that direction. We don't really have enough information to determine what separation means in that direction but on a first cut, we can take the 12,000 number as significant within itself. If we have 12,000 floors, each consisting of 1.5 acres, we would have a total "equivalent" acreage of 17,779 which is approximately 28 square miles. That is an astounding 28 square miles each or something slightly larger than 5 miles by 5 miles! This is for each person or "citizen of Heaven." That is a lot of land!!

Chapter 7.1

Engineering Accuracy of Scripture

1 Kings 7:23 (see also 2 Chronicles 4:2)
*"Now he made the sea of cast metal **ten cubits from brim to brim**, circular in form, and its height was five cubits, and **thirty cubits in circumference**."* (NAS)

Circumference: translated from 3 Hebrew words – Definitions:
- *Qvh*: a line - Strong's #6957b
- *Sabab*: to turn around or go a around - Strong's #5437
- *Sabib*: circuit or round about - Strong's #5439

"Sea" of Solomon's Temple

Somewhere around the 5th or 6th grade, most students learn to calculate the circumference (distance around) of a circle. Students are introduced to that amazing number π (Greek – pi). Circumference is easily calculated by using pi:

- π (pi) = 3.1415926…… (there is no end to the number of decimals that can be calculated)
- Circumference = π x Diameter
- Circumference of Solomon's Sea
  - Circumference = 10 cubits x π (3.1415926) = 31.41593 cubits

Wait a minute; the bible just said it was 30 cubits, not 31.4159. Who messed up? But, before we address that let's take in the grandeur of the Laver or wash basin or what is sometimes referred to as the "Sea." One of the largest of the Temple articles, the Sea is where much of the ceremonial washing took place. It is a whopping 15 feet in diameter and 7 ½ feet deep. Every morning, the priests were to ceremonial wash at the Sea, in a picture of our lives where every morning we are to approach God in our quite time, we wash in the "Water of the Word." Interestingly, when we get to heaven, as described in Revelation 5, we find ourselves standing on the "glassy sea." At that time, we will be in our resurrected bodies, no longer in need of daily cleansing, Jesus and His righteousness has been given to us. Fantastic! But, back on track.

Having long ago, quit worrying about "errors" in the bible, I find this a fascinating passage. Anyone capable of making Solomon's Temple, with massive stones weighing thousands of tons and fitting as close as a few thousandths of an inch, could certainly measure the diameter of the Sea well within less that a cubit. What is going on? Well, it turns out that a deeper dig into the Hebrew text produces some rich ore.

Shlomo Edward G. Belaga did some digging and his discovery was published by a paper from the Department of Mathematics of the Weizmann Institute. [195] In the ancient Hebrew texts of the scriptures, the scribes were extremely faithful in making copies. If there was something odd, like a spelling error, rather than make a correction, the text was copied exactly as the original but a note was made in the margin. The written variation was called a *kethiv* and the marginal annotation was referred to as a *gere*. Rabbis called these types of things a *remez* meaning "a hint of something deeper." What Belaga identified was that the word (translated circumference) *qav* (really two letters – q & v) was misspelled and was written instead as *qaveh* (adding another letter – h). Now, pay attention, but first a little quick background. Hebrew and Greek are

---

[195] "On the Rabbinical Approximation of Pi"; Boaz Tsaban and David Garber; copyright 1998; Academic press – find link from the math papers (1998) at http://www.cs.biu.ac.il/~tsaban/

special languages in that each letter has a numerical value (similar to Latin like X is 10 and M is 1,000). This is known a "gamatria" and some astounding things can be developed from the scriptures using gamatria (but that is the subject for another time). Looking at the numerical value of the Hebrew we find:

- Qav (qv in Hebrew) = q (100) + v (6) = 106
- Qaveh (qvh in Hebrew) = q (100) + v (6) + h (5) = 111

Being that this was highlighted by the Holy Spirit, lets compare the difference:

- Qaveh/Qav = 111/106 = 1.0471698...

What if we adjusted the scriptural 30 cubits by the adjustment highlighted by the Holy Spirit:

- 30 cubits x 1.0471698 (adjustment) = 31.41509 cubits
- Compare that with the calculated   31.41593 cubits
- Difference is 0.000832 cubits or about 0.0149 inches – that is only 15 thousants of an inch!!! (that's about the thickness of a few sheets of paper)

> **"Unbelievers have good questions, Christianity has Good Answers" - Norman Giesler**
> [196]

For a more complete description of this discovery, gamatria and many more fascinating finds check out "Cosmic Codes" by Chuck Missler. His book is one of the most outstanding I have ever read for deeper finds. He leads you on numerous exploratory dives so deep you will be getting the bends when you come up for a breath. [197]

How do you feel about this? Challenging isn't it. This specific subject generated the following thoughts:

- "This is just shameful behavior from the Inerrantist" [198] Website; "Inerrancy Exposed"

---

[196] "When Skeptics Ask"; Norman Giesler; Baker Books; copyright 1990- 8th printing – Feb 2003; page 14
[197] "Cosmic Codes"; Chuck Missler; Koinonia House Pub; copyright 1999; specifically page 286-290
[198] See Inerrancy Exposed: http://www.inerrancyexposed.com/molten_sea.html

- "[Not] all factual assertions are technically precise by modern standards (as opposed to accurate by ancient standards"; Normal Gielser [199] (great modern theologian and in the class I call the literalists)
- Missler - "Beyond simply these engineering insights from Solomon's day, there are more far-reaching implications of this passage:
    - 1) The Bible is reliable. The "errors" pointed our by skeptics usually derive from misunderstandings or trivial quibbles
    - 2) The numerical values of the letters are legitimate and apparently can carry hidden significance" [200]
- Sutliff – "I am in awe" [201]

*"For truly I say to you, until heaven and earth pass away, **not the smallest letter or stroke shall pass away** from the Law, until all is accomplished."* Matt 5:18

Perhaps there is more here than meets the eye.

---

[199] "Systematic Theology - Volume 1"; Norman Gielser; Bethany House Pub.; copyright 2002; page 237
[200] "Cosmic Codes"; page 290
[201] From memory – wait, I just thought of it.

Chapter 7.2

Television and CNN

Revelation 11:9

"*[8]And their dead bodies will lie in the street of the great city which mystically is called Sodom and Egypt, where also their Lord was crucified. [9]**Those from the peoples and tribes and tongues and nations will look at their dead bodies for three and a half days**, and will not permit their dead bodies to be laid in a tomb. [10]And those who dwell on the earth will rejoice over them and celebrate; and they will send gifts to one another, because these two prophets tormented those who dwell on the earth.*" (NAS)

Matthew 24:30

"*[29]"But immediately after the tribulation of those days THE SUN WILL BE DARKENED, AND THE MOON WILL NOT GIVE ITS LIGHT, AND THE STARS WILL FALL from the sky, and the powers of the heavens will be shaken. [30]"And then the sign of the Son of Man will appear in the sky, and then **all the tribes of the earth will mourn, and they will see** the SON OF MAN COMING ON THE CLOUDS OF THE SKY with power and great glory.*"

Has this little device, this inanimate object shaped Western Society more than anything else over the past 50 years? Has it had more influence in our culture than the Church? All this has happened on my watch.

World Wide Coverage

How does the entire world "see" a local event? How can peoples from the "tribes, tongues and nations" look at the dead bodies of the two witnesses who for the past 3 ½ years have proclaimed God's impending judgments to the world? Perhaps these verses anticipated the advent of the television and worldwide, real time satellite coverage that allows networks such as CNN and others to broadcast to the entire world events that are taking place on a local level.

It is my opinion that many of the atrocities of the last days will be broadcast live around the earth for all to see, but I do think the Return of Christ will be somewhat different. One day, Jesus, the Lord of Lords and the King of Kings will ride from heaven on a white horse (I think we just answered the question "are there animals in heaven?"), coming through hyperspace, and He will punch into the time-space continuum that we perceived and every eye will see Him on that day as He places His feet on the Mt. of Olives. Is television part of this? I'm not sure. Perhaps Christ will pass overhead of all the earth on His re-entry to Jerusalem.

Perhaps the machine that has brought lies and deceit to the entire globe for an extended period of time will broadcast live the good news of Christ's return, although sadly, it won't be well received news for most of the earth.

Chapter 7.3

Neutron Bomb

Zechariah 14:12-13
*"Now this will be the plague with which the LORD will strike all the peoples who have gone to war against Jerusalem; **their flesh will rot while they stand on their feet, and their eyes will rot in their sockets, and their tongue will rot in their mouth**. It will come about in that day that a great panic from the LORD will fall on them; and they will seize one another's hand, and the hand of one will be lifted against the hand of another... So also like this plague will be the plague on the horse, the mule, the camel, the donkey and all the cattle that will be in those camps. "* (NAS)

Death While Standing!

Students of the Scriptures can cite several plagues that God has brought in judgment throughout the history of man. We recall the death of the first born of Egypt, the plague of vipers and other medical type plagues that have brought life to an end. Typically these plagues are slow acting (Lev 26, Deut 28). However, what we see here in Zechariah 14 is destruction so rapid, it occurs while the victims are standing! It is instantaneous. Wow. We do recall Lot's wife who, with longing, looked back on the destruction of Sodom and Gomorrah and became a "pillar of salt". Certainly God, in a miraculous way can bring about instant destruction on those who oppose Him but we find that this passage is provocative in the sense that it parallels a description of the effects of a neutron bomb.

Also called Enhanced Radiation Bombs (ER weapons), they are small thermonuclear weapons specifically designed to kill people and leave everything else in tact. Destructive mechanism of most nuclear weapons is via an intense blast wave that levels everything in its path. In a tactical situation, if enemy forces are rapidly moving into a city for example, the use of most weapons can only stop the advance by "blowing up" everything including the city. A Neutron bomb is a small device that instead of a giant blast wave emits an extremely intense flux of neutrons. Neutron radiation is so high it penetrates buildings and armored vehicles at levels so high it destroys biological proteins and all living things are destroyed. Devices built by the US (although now destroyed) had lethal radius of less than a mile. Militarily, the good news is that only living biological things are destroyed and the buildings and other structures are left unharmed (except for those very close to ground zero). Because of the lack of an intense heat blast, the typical "mushroom cloud" is not present.

And what about those animals in verse 15? The horse, mule, camel and all the cattle. What did they do? Well, somehow they are caught up in all this and they meet the same demise and the people.

Countries part of the "Neutron Bomb Club" include Russia (see "red mercury") Israel and the United States (although ours are now destroyed) and possibly China.

Chapter 7.4

Smart Weapons

Jeremiah 50:9b

"....*Their **arrows will be like an expert warrior**, who does not return empty-handed*" (NAS)

Smart Arrows??

The grammar of this sentence implies that the "arrows" will be like "expert warriors", not that the arrows are sent by expert warriors. That is interesting. If this section is in reference to the future destruction of Babylon perhaps it anticipates the use of "Smart Weapons."

America's Advanced Cruise Missile (ACM - AGM-129) can be launched from any one of several aircraft including the B-52H bomber. It flies undetected (because of its stealth capability) over 1,865 miles to its pre-programmed target, strikes its target with the accuracy of 100 ft and then detonates an onboard W-80 thermonuclear warhead with a yield up to 150 k T [202] (recall that the bomb dropped on Hiroshima was about 15 k T) [That's called "Nuclear Deterrent"]

Arrow (Hebrew - *chets*); definition – arrow; Strong's #2671

Warrior (Hebrew – *gibbor*); definition – strong, migty, mighty man; Strong's #1368

Empty-handed (Hebrew – *reqam*) – definition – emptily, vainly or "Without Success" [203] ; Strong's #7387

---

[202] See Wikipedia: http://en.wikipedia.org/wiki/W80 and http://en.wikipedia.org/wiki/AGM-129_Advanced_Cruise_Missile for additional information

These "arrows" will hit their intended targets in an expert fashion, or with precision and accuracy doing the job they were sent to do. Bombs dropped during World War II were not very accurate being subject to a coarse alignment of the target from a plane flying at 10,000 feet, blowing winds and bomb aerodynamics. Smart missiles and weapons of today can be released at high altitudes (40,000 feet) and yet, because they have onboard computer processors and internal navigation systems, can strike even moving targets with accuracy of much less than 10 feet without any assistance from the shooter. "Fire and Forget" is a slogan of these types of systems.

Smart Bombs and weapons have given the modern war fighter an awesome capability and when his weapon is released, it is not in vain, it will strike it's target and accomplish the purpose for which it is intended. In the same way, when God speaks, His word goes out and does not return empty-handed or in vain (Isaiah 55:11 uses the same word *reqam*).

> God says *"So will My word be which goes forth from My mouth; It will not return to Me empty [reqam]"* Isaiah 55:11

---

[203] "New International Dictionary of Old Testament Theology & Exegesis – Vol 3"; Willem Van Gemeren – General Editor; Zondervan; copyright 1997; page 1106

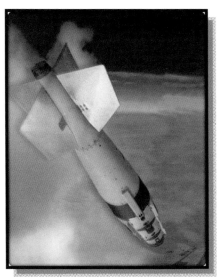

Boeing's Joint Direct Attack Munition – (JDAM) was used extensively during Operation Enduring Freedom and Operation Iraqi Freedom can be launched from an aircraft in relative safety up to 15 miles from the target in adverse weather delivering a MK 84 - 2,000 Lb. warhead with eye watering accuracy. [204]

Destruction of Babylon Past and Babylon Future.

Although some scholars disagree, the massive and complete destruction of the city of Babylon (described in Jeremiah 49-50; Isaiah 13-14 and Revelation 18) is foretold by God for the future in the end times. Some scholars see the destruction of Babylon described in Jeremiah 50 as a past event that occurred when Alexander the Great took over the city. However, some scholars noting that the ancient conquering was no where close to a complete destruction cite several parallels with Isaiah and Revelation concluding that Jeremiah is describing the same event as John in Revelation. In these passages, Babylon is completely destroyed never to be inhabited again (Jer 50:39). This view gains strength as Saddam Hussein began to re-build the city of Babylon several years ago.

God used ancient Babylon to conquer and destroy Judah and Jerusalem in punishment for their embracing of idols and their rejection of the living God. However, because of Babylon's harsh treatment of Israel, they too were in turn punished. Cyrus the Great and his general Darius (Medes) capture Babylon in a brilliant military move that involves damming up the river Euphrates that ran under the city wall and into the city. A small skilled force snuck under the city wall as the river flow decreased and they captured the city in one night without a battle. In fact, it was several days before most of the city folks realized that they had been conquered. Many years later, Alexander the Great also conquers

---

[204] See Boeing site: http://www.boeing.com/defense-space/missiles/jdam/docs/jdam_overview.pdf

the city but leaves it essentially completely intact. Alexander then uses the city as a key hub for his Greek empire. Neither these nor any other event in Babylon's past comes close to the complete and utter destruction described in Jeremiah 50 (see verses 39 & 40) where God likens Babylon's destruction to Sodom and Gomorrah.

US Marines in the City of Babylon, Iraq

Chapter 7.5

Destruction of all Flesh

Matthew 24:22
"And __unless those days had been cut short, no life would have been saved;__ but for the sake of the elect those days shall be cut short." (NAS)

Destruction of Life

As man catapulted himself into the 21st Century one of the unique positions that we have created for ourselves is the potential for the destruction of the entire population of the earth. Previously in history, as great armies attempted to bring the world into subjugation, life essentially continued on as always. Certainly under different rulers and

governments but life itself was never threatened. Today that is different. A few facts: [205]

- Even though nuclear weapons existed through the cold war, the chance of their use was actually very small (because of the stability provided by the "mutually assured destruction" outcome and the only two "game" players were basically stable.
- Today, there are a large number of players many who are rogue and or unstable in nature.
- There are 20 countries who have or shortly will have possession of nuclear weapons according to the International Atomic Energy Agency.
- Many possessors of nuclear weapons are not motivated by the typical territorial or monetary greed which has provided stability, but are devoutly religious

---

[205] Much of this information comes from: "Prophecy 20/20"; Dr. Chuck Missler; Nelson Books; Copyright 2006; Chapters 15 and 20.

- Popular Russian General Alexander Lebed stated on national television that he had 132 "suitcase nukes" manufactured, 85 of which are missing from inventory and unaccounted for.
- Over a total of 700 "suitcase nukes" were manufactured for the KGB, all of which are unaccounted for.
- Few scenarios' exist in which the detonation of a single device will not result in major escalation.
- Russia possesses about 6,000 nuclear warheads
- Saudi Arabia has installed 120 CSS-2 missiles which have a range of 1,500 km and they have 3 nuclear warheads for each missile

- A nuclear warhead detonated at aircraft altitude would generate an Electro-Magnetic Pulse (EMP) that is so strong it would render most all electronics completely useless. Senator Jon Kyle of the Senate Subcommittee of Terrorism, Technology and Homeland Security stated that the effect of a single such device would; "be to knock out already stressed power grids and other electrical systems over much if not all of the continental United States for much if not years.

CSS-2
DF-3

- In 1989 CIA Director William Webster stated that "at least ten countries" have been named as biological weapons countries
- Recently, when the *Majlis*, the Parliament of Iran, voted to pursue their nuclear program, 247 of the 290 approved by standing and shouting; "Death to America, death to Israel" – notice the order.
- The US Ohio Class Submarine is 560 feet long and can travel quietly at a speed of 20 kts. It is equipped with 24 nuclear missile launcher tubes which can place nuclear hardened targets at risk 6,000 miles away.

- The Russian Typhoon Class Submarine is 561 feet long and can travel in excess of 25 kts at unknown depths and for the first time in naval history, is *quieter* than the American counterpart. It is specifically designed to operate under the Artic and carries 20 missile tubes that launch the SS-20 nuclear missile which can carry 10 warheads each traveling a range estimated at 5,000 miles.

- The Typhoon sub is identified as the "Ultimate Strategic Weapon" and each sub can hold over 200 cities hostage.

"And I will send a fire on Magog, and among them that dwell carelessly in the isles; and they shall know that I am the Lord." Ezekiel 39:6

Magog = Soviet Russia
Carelessly (Hebrew *betach*) definition: in false confidence
Isle (Hebrew *yai 'ee*) definition: isle or coastland; and it is suggested from the previous passage to be a remote pleasant place.

"...unless those days had been cut short, no life would have been saved!"
Notice the subtlety. This is written in the past tense! Only an all knowing, all powerful sovereign God could make that statement.

> **National Destiny is dependent on National Behavior**
> **See 2 Chronicles 7:14**

7 – Engineering and Technology